Loneliness

The Experience of Emotional and Social Isolation

Foreword by David Riesman

The MIT Press
Cambridge, Massachusetts, and
London, England

Loneliness

The Experience of Emotional and Social Isolation

Robert S. Weiss

With contributions by
John Bowlby, C. Murray Parkes,
The Women's Group on Public Welfare,
Helena Z. Lopata, Morton M. Hunt,
Myrna M. Weissman and Eugene S. Paykel,
Peter Townsend

First MIT Press paperback edition, 1975

Copyright © 1973 by
The Massachusetts Institute of Technology

All rights reserved. No part of this book may be reproduced in any form or by any means, electronic or mechanical, including photocopying, recording, or by any information storage and retrieval system, without permission in writing from the publisher.

This book was set in linotype Baskerville, and printed and bound by Halliday Lithograph in the United States of America.

Library of Congress Cataloging in Publication Data

Weiss, Robert Stuart, 1925–
  Loneliness: the experience of emotional and social isolation.

  1. Loneliness. I. Title.
BF575.L7W44   158.2   73-9693
ISBN 978-0-262-23067-4 (hc : alk. paper)
ISBN 978-0-262-73041-9 (pb : alk. paper)

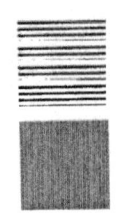

MIT Press
0262730413
WEISS
LONELINESS

Contents

Foreword by David Riesman   ix

Acknowledgments   xxiii

Introduction   1

1
The Study of Loneliness   7

2
The Nature of Loneliness   31

Introduction   33

Affectional Bonds:
Their Nature and Origin
by John Bowlby   38

Separation Anxiety:
An Aspect of the Search for a Lost Object
by C. Murray Parkes   53

3
Who Are the Lonely? 69

Introduction   71

Individuals Most Troubled by Loneliness
by The Women's Group on Public Welfare   79

4
The Loneliness of Emotional Isolation   87

Introduction   89

Loneliness: Forms and Components
by Helena Znaniecki Lopata   102

A Widower: Mr. Neilson   116

Alone, Alone, All, All Alone
by Morton M. Hunt   125

After the Breakup: Mrs. Graham   134

5
The Loneliness of Social Isolation   143

Introduction   145

Moving and Depression in Women
by Myrna M. Weissman and Eugene S. Paykel   154

An Uprooted Woman: Mrs. Phillips   165

Isolation and Loneliness in the Aged
by Peter Townsend   175

6
Responses to Loneliness 189

Introduction   191

Relying on One's Community: Mrs. Davis   197

Parents Without Partners
as a Supplementary Community   212

7
Conclusion:
Summary and Implications
for Further Study   225

Foreword

David Riesman

At the conclusion of this volume, Robert Weiss proffers some tentative advice to the lonely concerning how they might cope with their condition, and in my judgment what he says is sensible and humane. Yet he adds that he is almost embarrassed to offer advice to the lonely, as if to act like Ann Landers is somehow *infra dig* for a social scientist—though offering advice to the unemployed would not be so regarded. In some cruel and callous perspectives, which the victims themselves are apt to share, the lovelorn and the lonely—an overlapping but not identical group—seem somehow pathetic without being tragic, perhaps a bit like the fat boy who is supposed to be cheerful to help all the rest of us not feel any poignancy in his presence.

But in fact this is a deeply sad, even tragic, volume. Combining his own research and reflection with the work of others, Weiss builds upon an analytically and therapeutically useful distinction between two sorts of loneliness: *emotional* isolation, which results from the loss or lack of a truly intimate tie (usually with spouse, lover, parent, or child) and *social* isolation, the consequence of lacking a network of involvements with peers of some sort, be they fellow workers, kinfolk, neighbors, fellow hobbyists, or friends. The wounds of emotional isolation reflect the infant's tie (ordinarily) to the mother, the fear of abandonment, what used to be called a primordial tie; the closest ties have this quality, and the wounds of their absence can only be slowly healed, and then only when one finds a comparably intense involvement. The wife who outlives her husband (a common American phenomenon) is quite frequently in this position; there is no one to take his place.

In a penetrating essay, "On Social Regression,"[*] Philip Slater describes the efforts society makes to compel a sexually and emotionally intimate cross-sex couple to return, as it were, to ordinary social life with its peer ties and group responsibilities. The very term, *folie à deux*, indicates the social definition of such a presumably temporary withdrawal; Slater interprets marriage and other such rituals as society's verdict on the isolation preferred by the lovers. But Robert Weiss's material suggests that love is not enough. He reports studies that he and his colleagues have done of newcomer wives to the Boston metropolitan area who feel isolated in the absence of a social network even though they are deeply in love with their husbands and vice versa. To be sure, this is not Slater's case where the *pair* withdraws, for the man is bound by his job into a new network, and his work itself provides a vehicle for social integration, while the wife may find herself at loose ends even in a physically pleasant suburb where she does not know the name of the pharmacist, where the next-door neighbors may have children who are much younger or older than

---

[*] Philip E. Slater, "On Social Regression," *American Sociological Review*, Vol. 28, No. 3 (June 1963), pp. 339–364.

hers, or where for other reasons she cannot readily establish new ties.

American society gives many people the opportunity to calculate the potential benefits and losses from vertical mobility; guidance counselors can help people choose colleges and careers; even as adults, occupational counselors can advise them on moves to make, or avoid, in pursuit of a career. However, there is no similar organized system of advice concerning horizontal mobility and how to balance the age-old dialectic between the dangers of stagnation and lack of chances for self-development in staying home as against the risks of rootlessness or forlorn failure in moving elsewhere. In all societies there is a tug of war between the metaphorical incest of staying home, and the metaphorical uprooting of leaving home. Reading Weiss's pages, I was reminded of the excitement I felt when I was a college student wandering around what seemed the dangerous streets near the docks of Marseilles, realizing that no one in the world knew where I was—yet, at the same time, I had the comfort of knowing I had a family, a home to return to, a country to return to. What is adventure for those with a home base is deracination often for those who are without one and who cannot make use of America's plethora of second chances to discover a new one.

In the past, American men have frequently been willing to sacrifice their own comfort in favor of a chance for self-determination and self-expression; the comfort of their wives and children has been an ancillary consideration. The cultural verdict until recently on wives who held their husbands back, who were sticky and resistant to moves, has been unsympathetic. Indeed, women are in general not encouraged by social institutions rationally to calculate what geographical moves will benefit them. Unmarried women seldom realize that they may remain spinsters in Boston while they might find husbands in Alaska or Seattle; though many women do think in this way and are encouraged by their kinfolk to do so, they often regard such thinking as somehow unromantic, even unfeminine. Similarly, when bereaved, they may find it difficult to become calculating as to where their best chances are for remarriage and reintegration into a network such as was previously provided by the life of the couple. These things are just supposed to happen, and women's unconscious may either protect or betray them as the case may be.

As divorce becomes more prevalent, and as more young women are the daughters of divorced parents, marriage itself may come to seem to many women more risky than its alternatives. Indeed, Weiss suggests that a woman who has had an affair can resume a normal social life more readily than one who has been divorced or widowed and who is thereby cut off from the sociability of married couples: ending a marriage unsettles friendships all around, whereas ending an affair does not. (See in this connection the essay by Helena Lopata in this volume.) I suppose there are circles of the fashionably emancipated where what I have just said is not so, and little distinction is drawn between couples who are married and couples who are living together.

However, it is also clear from the material in this book that life in a commune does not end problems of loneliness; relations may be severed and people left lonely even in the midst of the collectivity, and perhaps all the more bitter because one is daily reminded of what one has lost. Furthermore, the commune, like a new family, has its own stickiness, perhaps intensified when it is dominated by an egalitarian ethos that minimizes the distinctive abilities and interests of its members.*

In her autobiography, *Blackberry Winter,* Margaret Mead describes how her experience of being excluded from the sorority life at DePauw affected her judgment of what it meant to exclude and to be excluded, and gave her empathy in later life toward those who were lonely or prone to suicide.† Weiss observes there are people who turn loneliness into a kind of grandeur, prideful in isolation, rejecting in order not to be rejected. But most Americans tend, he suggests, to repress remembrance of the experience of loneliness when we are not at the moment lonely, so that it is difficult to identify with those who suffer from the disease—or not to tell them, as with those who suffer from depression, to snap out of it, or to get around and meet people. Yet as self-consciousness grows about the costs of geographic mobility, it is possible to imagine a "union" of wives and children being formed to set up collective moral roadblocks against their husbands' mobility; this could occur even while, among the liberated, men now are sometimes subordinating their own careers and moving (or staying put) in order to advance the wife's career. Indeed, women may be turning against the American Dream

---
* See Jo Freeman, "The Tyranny of Structurelessness," *Berkeley Journal of Sociology,* Vol. XVII (1972–73), pp. 151–164.
† See Margaret Mead, *Blackberry Winter: My Earlier Years* (New York: William Morrow and Company, 1972), pp. 92 et seq.

of upward mobility for their husbands and even for themselves where, as so often, this involves horizontal mobility. And yet, the difficulty of forming any such union of the sedentary, despite all the current talk about community and "urban villages" lies in the fact that, even if one stays put, other people around one move, so that there is no way to count on stability. Moreover, what may be stability for one member of the family may be entrapment for another—spouses of course do not feel justified in trapping each other, even if they can get away with it, any more than parents feel justified in keeping their adult children at home.

The book makes clear how often we Americans blame ourselves for what goes amiss in our lives; yet chance plays a tremendous part, especially but not only for those who have little ability to plan. Consider the case of Mrs. Phillips reported here. Her move from an uncongenial to a congenial suburb provided an extraordinary transformation in Mrs. Phillips's whole outlook on life. Her earlier dependence on her husband and daughter, precisely by trapping them, threatened the dependence itself, and hence the very bedrock of Mrs. Phillips's emotional integration, for in a characteristic vicious circle, the closer she clung, the more she risked alienating those to whom she clung. What she needed, as events showed, was not a change of character, but a change of setting. In the old location, a neighbor to whom she had perforce turned chanced to be an alcoholic; in the new neighborhood, a church, the Red Cross, the League of Women Voters, all quickly brought her into a network of peers. It is often thought that women need women to talk to, that blacks need blacks, and so on. Mrs. Phillips remarked: "Women need a woman to talk to, they really do. It's because women understand women . . ." Many women undoubtedly need other women to talk to, but I question the implication that only women understand women. For instance, I am inclined to think that Robert Weiss understands women; I sometimes hope that I do; I deeply believe in vicarious understanding, and having recently been steeped in George Eliot's novels, I do not believe that the converse holds, that women cannot understand men, or indeed that only insiders, by whatever social definition, understand other insiders. But it is true in America that cross-sex, nonsexual ties of deep intimacy are rare and precarious; we do not for the most part find them customary or comfortable. In part this is because we conventionally assume that the erotic elements in such a tie will necessarily take active sexual form.* In the slum sex code described long ago by William F. Whyte, Jr., it was taken for granted that a man and a woman were never alone together without the man's trying to "take ad-

---

* When the late President Johnson found in my friend and colleague Doris Kearns a confidante who could interpret for him the contempt he faced from younger and academic people, while at the same time sympathizing with his aspirations and admiring his accomplishments in domestic affairs, many observers assumed that there must be a sexual tie between these two, as if there could not be such intensity without that. I have sometimes wondered whether the declosetting of male homosexuals would produce a cadre of men who could be escorts for otherwise isolated women without the risk of sexual misinterpretation or temptation on either side. Of course, it is only some male homosexuals who can enjoy the company of women without feeling called upon to prove their masculinity, or the defend themselves against women.

vantage" of the woman sexually; nice women needed chaperones. Among the educated, the assumption is that if a woman is really fond of a man, fondness is likely to be given sexual expression as the best and, in many circles, the only proof of love. New styles of coresidential living in our colleges may change these assumptions, as may also be happening in some of the communes, where men and women may learn to be comfortably and tenderly together, without traditional inhibition and without chaperonage, and without the assumption that sexual intercourse will be the usual outcome. It remains to be seen whether these apparent changes will endure.

While much of the material in the book is concerned with the social isolation of women, Weiss is aware that there are contexts where men may suffer more than women from emotional isolation. For example, because women are more active than men in keeping up kin ties and especially ties with their children, fathers may find that in the absence of their wives, they have lost the ties to their children at the same time that they may also have lost through retirement the tie to any colleague group at work. Since men are, even more than women, expected to be stoical and not to impose their emotional burdens on others, they may not be able to share their sense of loss and deprivation.

Growing awareness of these traumas has led some observers to see American mobility as a kind of semivoluntary urban renewal, not renewal but destruction of community and neighborhood. And among many young, educated people today, there appears to be a great longing for community, and an unwillingness to join organizational networks that will force them to move, whether these are the military or academic professions or large business corporations. I find it hard to imagine Americans continuing to run an economy which is part of the world market, and which supports over 200 million people with ever-rising expectations, without there being a great deal of horizontal and vertical mobility as people sort themselves out to try to match their abilities to available opportunities, even though I can imagine a good deal more decentralization of economic and educational as well as cultural opportunities than exists at present. Nor does Robert Weiss see any prospect of turning the American motion picture into a still photograph.

But it does seem possible to reduce somewhat the extravagant expectations of many Americans about what life is supposed to offer us as proper Americans. A few years ago, C. Vann Woodward contended that Southerners had suffered defeat in war and had thus known tragedy and fatality in a way then unfamiliar to the North. The observation surely holds for some reflective Southerners such as Woodward himself, but I have not noticed that Southerners have been less prone to the escalation of expectations than the rest of us concerning victory over evil or distress either abroad or at home. Robert Weiss offers us no guide as to how Americans can become more realistic about the human condition. But he understands that, because as Americans we are supposed to be cheerful, competent, successful, and happy, we suffer not only from terrible pangs of loneliness, but from the secondary pangs of not leading the kind of life, filled with all the proper psychic accouterments, that bountiful Americans are supposed to lead. Lee Rainwater has found, in studying the relativity of poverty in America, that people who earn less than half the median income feel poor, whatever their absolute situation; those whose emotional poverty line is below the expected level may feel this second pang of shame at being lonely, which then creates a vicious circle of self-doubt and self-pity, as if to be lonely is some sort of un-American inactivity.

My great-grandmother, who had a number of children, and whose husband died when she was thirty-five, lived on until she was one hundred and four. She lived in the same townhouse in Philadelphia, owning a coach and pair until there weren't any more coachmen, welcoming her children and grandchildren and then great-grandchildren on birthdays and other ceremonial occasions, but living most of her life with only the company of servants. As I recall her, she did not feel aggrieved; she kept her head high, her values seemingly unchanged, her expectations by our contemporary standards, small. The fact of being alone was hard, but then she had not learned any other lesson than that life was hard.

The theologian Krister Stendahl once remarked that if one is seeking to console a mother grieving for the death of a child, it helps to believe in the Devil. Societies where the belief in witchcraft is prevalent, or indeed our own society when it believed in immortality, found the blows of fate, if not easier to bear, at least lacking in that secondary impact of the belief that only oneself was to blame—a problem that confronted Job and his tactless comforters. We have seen in the United States in recent years the organization of a politicized sense of grievance among many people who would once have blamed themselves for deviance or stigma. People who realize themselves as victimized collect around each other, gather injustices, and turn the fact of having been victimized into a weapon against their quondam oppressors. In a society preoccupied with fairness, one could conceive of a social-science fiction, analogous to Michael Young's *The Rise of the Meritocracy*, in which those who lacked the average fund of sociability would attack those who had "too many" friends; there is an element of this in the attack on cliques in school, or on fraternities and sororities in college, even when these do not discriminate along obvious lines of racial or ethnic cleavage.

From Weiss's data, it is clear that the lonely often do feel anger—including what they recognize to be an irrational anger—against a deceased spouse who has left them bereft, as well as an understandable or more readily rationalized anger against a living relative or former spouse who has decamped. While the parents of retarded children can mobilize effectively to get help for such children in general, turning their guilt and grievance into a social movement, it is hard to imagine lonely people, the bereft ones, forming a similar social movement in search of some sort of political or cultural redress. For the lack of social integration, they can blame the strains and stresses of American mobility in the way already indicated; but out of the emotional isolation of bereavement, they cannot create a crusade. Indeed, so great is the shame of the lonely, causing them to withdraw further out of fear of additional experiences of loss, that they are wary of each other's company—a bit like Groucho Marx, who believed that any club that admitted him could not be worth joining.

Hence the embarrassment and transiency of members of Parents Without Partners.

Robert Weiss asks us to become more self-conscious about the epidemiology of social isolation, to discover on the one hand who are the people most at risk (such as newcomer housewives in certain kinds of neighborhoods) and, eventually, what character types may be most prone to both the emotional and social aspects of loneliness. It is possible to develop ancillary networks, a kind of psychological social security, for various sorts of social isolation. Parents Without Partners, already mentioned, is an organization whose overt aim is to help people psychologically in the same boat, and whose tacit aim is to help them meet each other so as to repair their emotional lacunae. Because we do not live in extended families, we need such ancillary groups.

Robert Weiss's counsel at the end is that, since society cannot make restitution for bereavement and grief, individuals should plan ahead to cope with its vicissitudes and terrors. As a college teacher, I see this as a problem in education. College should be a time for planning ahead. I urge on students that they take out career insurance against the chances and mischances of life, organizing their undergraduate years so that they emerge with the confidence born of competence, that if one track fails they can find another: having learned one language, they can more easily learn others, or learn other demanding skills that will open the way to still others. For example, I often urge on Radcliffe students that, instead of majoring in English, they major in a language and literature such as Japanese or Russian so they would have access to a great literature and culture, but also might gain employment opportunities not open to the typical English majors, who will be competing for jobs as a *Fortune* magazine researcher or a publisher's assistant. And I urge this especially on women students because, as things are in spite of any progress made by the women's movement, women are still more likely than men to find themselves waylaid in the occupational world; they can no more afford spontaneity in curriculum than in contraception.

I also urge on students of both sexes that they employ their college years to learn a lifelong sport, a lifelong musical instrument, and other lifelong interests that may stand them in good stead, whatever fate befalls them in later life. Many of the lonely ones of whom there are vignettes in this volume have no interests beyond the ordinary; they can watch TV like anybody else, perhaps play cards like anybody else, have drinks in a bar like anybody else—but none of these activities provides more than casual access to a network of like-minded people who could become friends and, in the luck of the draw, potential mates. Young people believe that they should be loved for themselves alone, almost as if for their protoplasmic existence; to cultivate qualities that would make them attractive to others would seem inauthentic, even gross. Yet only saints and masochists are not "unfair" when it comes to choosing friends and lovers. Since we do need others as part of our human condition, we need to think when we are young about how we can still have something to give others when we are old, what we will have to offer in terms of inner resource and outgoing interest. It is clear from Weiss's materials that the sheer hunger for others is an off-putting trait, and that emotional isolation is best cured not by going about it too strenuously, however great the loss which gave rise to it. In that sense, it is like happiness, whose direct pursuit is self-defeating; for happiness, like emotional integration, is often the by-product of other activities.

Acknowledgments

Original materials presented in this book are largely based on studies conducted at Harvard Medical School's Laboratory of Community Psychiatry. I would like here to acknowledge the contributions of my colleagues in these studies: Dr. Peggy Golde, Dr. Elizabeth Harvey, Mrs. Beatrice Horwitz, Dr. Richard S. Maisel, Dr. Colin M. Parkes, and Mrs. Emily Sullivan. I would like also to acknowledge the importance to my thinking of participation in a seminar conducted by Dr. John Bowlby of the Tavistock Centre in London and of discussions with Dr. Carroll Bourg of Fisk University. I want to thank the Director of the Laboratory of Community Psychiatry, Dr. Gerald Caplan, for his unfailing support. I want to thank him and also Dr. Arlene K. Daniels and Mr. Peter Marris for helpful comments on the manuscript. Finally, I want to thank Mrs. Mary Coffey for typing and retyping.

Some of the interview materials were collected under a grant from the Department of Health, Education, and Welfare, Social and Rehabilitation Service. Work on the manuscript was supported by a National Institute of Mental Health Research Scientist Development Award.

Introduction

Loneliness is among the most common distresses. In one survey of a reasonably representative sample of Americans, a quarter of those interviewed said they had suffered from loneliness within the past few weeks. In another survey, about one in nine of those interviewed said they had suffered from severe loneliness as recently as the preceding week.[1] Severe loneliness appears to be almost as prevalent as colds during the winter.[2]

For a condition so pervasive, loneliness has received remarkably little professional attention. In 1959 Frieda Fromm-Reichmann noted that loneliness was "not even mentioned in most psychiatric textbooks."[3] Ten years later the psychiatrist P. Herbert Leiderman reported that little had changed: "One might reasonably expect loneliness to be mentioned frequently in the psychiatric literature . . . [but] examination of this literature reveals few papers on this subject."[4] One might add that it is not only in the psychiatric literature that loneliness stands as a neglected topic; there are even fewer discussions of loneliness in the literature of psychology and sociology.[5]

Especially lacking are studies that would identify the various expressions of the ordinary loneliness that is so widespread an experience and would show how these expressions relate to the causes of loneliness. We are lacking, in short, in studies that would describe what loneliness is and explain why it is that way.

In this book I have brought together papers which do attempt to capture the phenomena of loneliness or to provide some explanation for those phenomena. I have added in introductions and elsewhere my own understanding of the nature of loneliness. And where it was appropriate I have also provided case materials that might illustrate—but more, might *illuminate*—the descriptive and theoretical accounts.[6]

Following these presentations I have tried to deal with the issue of how loneliness may be managed. I have described in some detail the relative merits of relying on existent networks and of entrance into new, supplementary, networks. And finally I have, with some discomfort, suggested what might be useful advice for at least some among the lonely.

The book is organized in seven sections. The first considers possible explanations for the neglect loneliness has heretofore suffered in the professional journals and also attempts to specify the condition that might be described, in ordinary life, as "loneliness." The next presents two papers that together may suggest mechanisms underlying at least one form of loneliness, if not loneliness as a generic experience. The third section presents a discussion of situations in which loneliness seems commonly found. Authored by an English fact-finding committee, it suggests that loneliness is a possibility in virtually every life. The fourth section turns to the loneliness of emotional isolation and examines its expression among those who have lost someone to whom they were emotionally attached. The fifth section considers the loneliness of social isolation, focusing on the experience of geographical uprooting. This section also examines the consequences of the increasing isolation that afflicts many old people. The sixth section considers the resources available to the lonely; it contrasts the possible contributions of an individual's existent community of family and friends with those that may be made by a supplementary community entered to compensate for the inadequacies of the existent community. The last section reviews briefly what has earlier been said about loneliness, attempts to outline some of the important issues yet to be dealt with, and, as was noted above, offers some suggestions for the management of loneliness.

This book is primarily addressed to others in the social sciences who share with me an interest in loneliness as an area for study and to professional clinicians who may find value for their work in an increased understanding of loneliness. But I also hope this book will be useful to individuals who now or in the future may be troubled by loneliness, a group that includes, I suspect, all of us. Loneliness is entirely natural in certain situations, yet it is so easy to think of it as weakness or self-indulgence, so easy to say that since one is suffering no physical pain or obvious privation, it should be possible to shrug off one's loneliness, even to label it solitude and thereupon enjoy it. At least, so goes the too frequent advice, one ought not to let oneself become caught up in self-pity: use the time alone to perform household chores or to improve your mind. The lonely are apt to hear this advice from others, but even if they do not, they very likely will offer it to themselves. And they, like others, will condemn themselves if they cannot shake off their loneliness and attend to something else. I hope this book, by its discussion of the causes and nature of loneliness, may lead the lonely as well as others to greater recognition of the force of loneliness as well as its normality under appropriate circumstances. And I hope that these recognitions may in turn support greater sympathy for those exposed to loneliness by the course their lives have taken.

NOTES

1. These studies are discussed at greater length in the first section.
2. According to the article on colds in the *Encyclopaedia Britannica*, 1964, a survey conducted by the American Institute of Public Opinion during a November week found that "approximately one person in seven throughout the country was afflicted with a cold."
3. Frieda Fromm-Reichmann, "Loneliness," *Psychiatry* 22, no. 1 (January 1959): 1.
4. P. Herbert Leiderman, "Loneliness: a psychodynamic interpretation," in *Aspects of Depression*, edited by Edwin S. Shneidman and Magno J. Ortega (Boston: Little, Brown and Co., 1969), p. 155.
5. Sociologists have given a great deal of attention to "alienation," by which most mean something like the social or psychological estrangement of an individual from an activity or social form with which he is nevertheless at least nominally associated. There seems to be very little overlap between the phenomena considered in discussions of alienation and the experience of loneliness. See *Social Aspects of Alienation: An Annotated Bibliography* by Mary H. Lystad (Washington: National Institute of Mental Health, 1969). For a pioneering discussion of loneliness by a sociologist see Claude C. Bowman, "Loneliness and social change," *American Journal of Psychiatry* 112 (1955).
6. The reports are derived from interviews averaging two hours in length conducted as contributions to studies of bereavement, marital separation, and a pilot study of uprooting. These studies were part of the research program of the Laboratory of Community Psychia-

try, Harvard Medical School. The bereavement study will be reported in a forthcoming book by Ira O. Glick, Colin M. Parkes, and Robert S. Weiss, *The First Year of Bereavement* (New York: John Wiley). Materials regarding marital separation will be reported in part in a forthcoming book by Robert S. Weiss, *Marital Separation* (New York: Basic Books).

1

The Study
of Loneliness

Loneliness is a condition that is widely distributed and severely distressing. Yet only a handful of psychiatrists, psychologists, and sociologists have studied the ordinary loneliness of ordinary people. Sullivan, the great American psychiatrist, is among the very few who have done so and among the very few in any of the social sciences who have attempted a description of the symptomatology of loneliness. His description is brief and sketchy, but nevertheless notably perceptive. In particular he commented on the "driving force" of loneliness—a force great enough, he pointed out, to cause people who were normally painfully shy to aggressively seek social activity. He concluded that "The fact that loneliness will lead to integrations in the face of severe anxiety automatically means that loneliness in itself is more terrible than anxiety." [1] Others who have observed the pressures under which the lonely seem to act by and large have agreed with Sullivan's appraisal.[2]

Why, then, has there been so little research on loneliness? Loneliness is much more often commented on by songwriters than by social scientists. One psychiatrist has suggested that we neglect loneliness because we have no theory with which to begin to cope with its manifestations.[3] There may be some merit in this position; scientific attention may be directed in part by the emphases of theory and the established preoccupations of the field. But Frieda Fromm-Reichmann noted that at least one reason that we have no very good theory about loneliness is that we have studied it so little. She suggested that the absence of attention to loneliness was to be explained not by the challenge loneliness presented to understanding but rather by the threat it presented to well-being. She said that loneliness is "such a painful, frightening experience that people will do practically everything to avoid it." [4]

Fromm-Reichmann's explanation is appealing but seems not to go far enough. There has for some time now been active research interest in the sometimes excruciatingly painful phenomena of grief and the intensely anxiety-provoking phenomena of dying,[5] and loneliness would not seem to be more frightening than these conditions. There would seem to be some additional quality in loneliness that leads to its neglect.

Many of us severely underestimate our own past experience with loneliness and as a result underestimate the role it has played in the lives of others. The observation that times of loneliness are later difficult to recall has been made by both Sullivan and Fromm-Reichmann. Sullivan believed that loneliness was an experience so different from the ordinary that its intensity could later not be entirely credited. He said it was "an experience which has been so terrible that it practically baffles clear recall." [6] Fromm-Reichmann believed that there was active rejection of the memory of loneliness, and not simply passive inability to recall. She believed that many of those who had once been lonely were aware that memory of that state would be threatening to their current well-being.

She said, "It is so frightening and uncanny in character that they [those who have once suffered loneliness] try to dissociate the memory of what it was like and even the fear of it." [7]

I have occasionally asked individuals who were not at the moment lonely to recall for me times when they had been. If I knew that a year or so earlier they had moved into a new community where they had had no friends, or that until the last few months they had been without an intimate, I pressed them to remember how they had felt during these periods of relational insufficiency. More than once I have been told something like, "Yes, I suppose I was lonely. But I wasn't *myself* then." I think this is a most suggestive response. It implies that an individual when lonely maintains an organization of emotions, self-definitions, and definitions of his or her relations to others, which is quite different from the one he maintains when not lonely. Asked at a time when he is not lonely to remember back to when he was lonely, he may protest that the person he is at the moment has never been lonely and that in the lonely past "I wasn't myself." The self associated with the absence of loneliness is a different one from the self associated with loneliness: it is more engaged by a range of interests, more confident, more secure, more self-satisfied. To someone in this state the earlier lonely self— tense, restless, unable to concentrate, *driven*—must seem an aberration.

As an implication of the foregoing we might expect that those who are not at the moment lonely will have little empathy for those who are, even if in the recent past they had been lonely themselves. If they had earlier been lonely, they now have no access to the self that experienced the loneliness;

furthermore, they very likely prefer that things remain that way. In consequence they are likely to respond to those who are currently lonely with absence of understanding and perhaps irritation.

Professionals in research and treatment, if they have dealt with their own past experiences of loneliness in this way, might also prefer not to disturb their current emotional arrangements. To maintain their current feelings of well-being, they too might be impatient with the problem of loneliness. They might be willing to consider loneliness in an exotic form —the loneliness of the mentally ill or of the Arctic explorer or the alienation of marginal man. But they would be made uncomfortable by the loneliness that is potential in the everyday life of everyone.

The frequency and intensity of loneliness are not only underestimated but the lonely themselves tend to be disparaged. It seems easy to blame their loneliness on their frailties and to accept this fault-finding as explanation. Our image of the lonely often casts them as justifiably rejected: as people who are unattractive, shy, intentionally reclusive, undignified in their complaints, self-absorbed, self-pitying. We may go further and suppose that chronic loneliness must to some extent be chosen. Surely, we might argue, it is easy enough to be acceptable to others. All that is necessary is to be pleasant, outgoing, interested in the others rather than in oneself. Why can't the lonely change? They must find a perverse gratification in loneliness; perhaps loneliness, despite its pain, permits them to continue a self-protective isolation or provides them with an emotional handicap that forces handouts of pity from those with whom they interact. Thoughts like these may justify professional as well as lay impatience with the lonely.[8]

There may be some small merit in this characterological theory of loneliness, as we shall later note. But there is also implicit in it a rationalization for rejection of the lonely and of the problem of loneliness. Each is pictured as easy to understand: the lonely are people who move against others or away from others and of course they then feel bad because they are alone. Along these lines, advice for the lonely would seem obvious: be pleasant, outgoing, interested in others; meet people; become part of things. If the lonely cannot behave in these ways, then they ought to enter psychotherapy, change, learn to be more outgoing.

Yet for those who suffer from loneliness, advice of this sort often seems oddly beside the point. There may seem to them to be something in loneliness that is "uncanny," to use Fromm-Reichmann's word. It is peculiarly insistent; no matter how much those who are lonely would like to shake it off, no matter how much they may berate themselves for permitting it to overcome them, they find themselves possessed by it. No matter how devotedly they may count their other blessings, no matter how determined they may be to put their minds to other things, the loneliness remains, an almost eerie affliction of their spirits.

Loneliness is not simply a desire for company, any company; rather it yields only to very specific forms of relationship. Loneliness is often uninterrupted by social activity; the social activity may feel "out there," in no way engaging the individual's emotions. It can even make matters worse. However the responsiveness of loneliness to just the right sort of relationship with others is absolutely remarkable. Given the establishment of these relationships, loneliness will vanish abruptly and without trace, as though it never had existed. There is no gradual recovery, no getting over it bit by bit. When it ends, it ends suddenly; one was lonely, one is not any more.

LONELINESS AND OTHER CONDITIONS

What do we mean by loneliness? The word has been used to describe a number of different conditions, even as other words, including *depression* and *grief,* have been used to describe conditions that would seem to have some affinity with loneliness.

Sometimes the term *loneliness* has been used to describe a not at all disagreeable condition in which a sense of one's separateness from others offers "a way back to oneself." [9] This sort of loneliness refers to a time in which one is not only alone but also able to use one's aloneness to recognize with awesome clarity both one's ineradicable separateness from all else and one's fundamental connectedness. It is a time of almost excruciating awareness in which one sees clearly the fundamental facts of one's small but unique place in the ultimate scheme, after which one can recognize one's true self and begin to be that true self.

I do not doubt that this experience occurs: that there are times when being alone gives rise to this awesome awareness of oneself and one's world. Some individuals may be able to transmute the intense discomfort of ordinary loneliness into this exalted state. But the state, even if it begins in ordinary loneliness, is different from the experience described to my colleagues and me in our studies of loneliness in ordinary life.

The loneliness we have been told of is gnawing rather than ennobling, a chronic distress without redeeming features.

Another condition that may be described as loneliness is unwanted individuation: being separated off from parents and others to fend for oneself, not just in the sense of becoming responsible for oneself but also in the sense of being and developing as a separate self.[10] Again, although this condition may be related to what most of us experience as loneliness, it does not appear to be quite the same thing. Nor is the existentialist notion of the ultimate loneliness of each of us in deciding and evaluating our course in life the same thing.

The condition discussed in this book is the one Sullivan described as "the exceedingly unpleasant and driving experience connected with inadequate discharge of the need for human intimacy."[11] This common, if perplexing, condition is the only one we have had reported to us in our studies of loneliness in ordinary life, excerpts from which are presented later in this book. The other forms of loneliness I have just noted would appear from our studies to be fairly rare states. They are not the loneliness experienced by those who are bereaved or divorced or uprooted.

Ordinary loneliness is uniformly distressing. It may be useful to distinguish it from other forms of distress. To begin with, it is different from what is usually described as depression. In loneliness there is a drive to rid oneself of one's distress by integrating a new relationship or regaining a lost one; in depression there is instead a surrender to it. The lonely are driven to find others, and if they find the right others, they change and are no longer lonely. The depressed are often unwilling to impose their unhappiness on others; in any event their feelings cannot be reached by relationships, old or new.[12]

Loneliness is also distinct from grief. The term *grief* may be used in a number of ways but perhaps is best used to describe the syndrome of shock, protest, anger, and painful, searing sadness, which is produced by traumatic loss.[13] Loneliness often is a component of this syndrome; however it is a reaction to the *absence* of the cherished figure rather than to the experience of its loss. We would expect every other aspect of grief to subside as time goes on: shock might be expected to disappear, protest to be muted, anger and sadness to diminish. But loneliness, so long as no new relationship is formed to replace what has been lost, might be expected to continue.

ORDINARY LONELINESS

Research on the nature of ordinary loneliness is as yet fragmentary. Surveys have generated useful statistics regarding the proportions of individuals in various demographic categories who declare themselves to be lonely, but to my knowledge none has investigated the reasons for loneliness, the conditions under which loneliness occurs, or the subjective experience of loneliness. We do have, however, case studies of individuals living in conditions likely to give rise to loneliness. These describe individuals who have been widowed, who have separated from or divorced a spouse, who have entered into a new community, or who have suffered the loss of intimates which is one of the afflictions of advanced age. On the basis of these studies we can develop some initial understandings of loneliness.

The dictionary definition of loneliness is not very useful. This is how Webster's defines the term: ". . . A state of dejection or grief caused by the condition of being alone..."[14] To be sure, no one who is lonely would consider himself happy, and to this extent Webster's is correct in associating loneliness with dejection and grief. But the definition is misleading in asserting that loneliness *is* dejection or grief; loneliness is quite different from these conditions, as has been noted earlier. More important, the definition is misleading in asserting that loneliness is "caused by the condition of being alone." On this point the case study materials we have collected are unambiguous. Loneliness is caused not by being alone but by being without some definite needed relationship or set of relationships.

Only those who are not lonely suppose that loneliness can be cured merely by ending aloneness. Not only is random sociability no antidote to loneliness, but under some circumstances it can exacerbate it; someone who is not married and in consequence feels outside the society of settled family life may find that being with married couples only intensifies his or her feelings of marginality, of having no valid place. A widower, some of whose experiences are described in a later chapter, said about an evening with married friends, "It's like being a fifth wheel."

Loneliness appears always to be a response to the absence of some particular type of relationship or, more accurately, a response to the absence of some particular relational provision. In many instances it is a response to the absence of the provisions of a close, indeed intimate, attachment. It may also be a response to the absence of the provisions of meaningful friendships, collegial relationships, or other linkages to a coherent community. These seem to be the most common forms of loneliness, but there may be others as well; conceivably, some parents whose children have left home may feel the absence of the distinctive provisions of the relationship one maintains with those one has nurtured. And at Christmas time, especially, many of those who are unable to join with kin feel distressed by the separation, for Christmas is a time of reaffirmation by kin of their fundamental commitment to one another.[15]

All these instances of conditions giving rise to loneliness support the presumption that loneliness is a response to relational deficit. Although each syndrome of response to specific relational deficit appears to be unique in some respects, each appears to include certain common symptoms, just as any infection may have both unique symptoms by which it can be distinguished from other infections and also shared symptoms such as fever. All loneliness syndromes would seem to give rise to yearning for the relationship—an intimacy, a friendship, a relationship with kin—that would provide whatever is at the moment insufficient. All may be able to produce the driving restlessness of which Sullivan spoke. And all may induce impatience or irritability with relationships that seem to impede access to the desired relationship. Insofar as those symptoms seem to be part of any experience of loneliness one may speak of "loneliness" as a single condition.

Different forms of loneliness are, however, responsive to different remedies. We have repeatedly found in our studies that a form of loneliness that appears in the absence of a close emotional attachment, which we characterize as "the loneliness of emotional isolation," can only be remedied by the integration of another emotional attachment or the reintegration of the one that had been lost.[16] Evidence that the loneliness of emotional isolation cannot be dissolved by entrance into other sorts of relationships, perhaps especially new friendships, is repeatedly rediscovered by new members of the Parents Without Partners organization. New members often are attracted to that organization because they are lonely and hope membership will allay the loneliness. Within the organization they may form new friendships or take on new responsibilities, but unless they also form a single intense relationship, one which in some ways makes the same provisions as the marriage they no longer have, they remain lonely.

Conversely, we have found that the form of loneliness associated with the absence of an engaging social network—the "loneliness of social isolation"—can be remedied only by access to such a network. This was demonstrated for us in a pilot study of couples who had moved to the Boston region from at least two states away.[17] The wives in these couples tended for a time to have "newcomer blues"; they felt out of place and unwanted in their new community and were deeply homesick for their former one. Their husbands, no matter how close the marriage, were of little help. The husbands did not share their wives' distress since they had entered a ready-made community at their workplace. Furthermore, the husbands' attention and energies were absorbed by their efforts to become established in their new jobs. But even when the husbands did seem able in a limited way to understand and to sympathize, the wives continued to be lonely for friends and acquaintances who would share their interests as their husbands did not. They wanted access to a network of women with whom they might establish and then discuss issues of common concern: shopping, home management, the developing lives of their children and, of course, one another. Though the newcomer wife might be content in her marriage, social isolation nevertheless made her painfully lonely, and her loneliness ended only when she found an accepting—and acceptable—community.

The complex of symptoms of the loneliness of emotional isolation are in the main different from those of the loneliness of social isolation, although there is in each the same driving restlessness and the same yearning for the missing relational provisions. The complex of symptoms associated with the loneliness of emotional isolation is strongly reminiscent of the distress of the small child who fears that he has been abandoned by his parents. On the other hand, the symptoms associated with the loneliness of social isolation are like the boredom, feelings of exclusion, and feelings of marginality of the small child whose friends are all away. We might reasonably suspect that the loneliness states of adults are developments of the earlier childhood states. They may have been modified by the new strengths and understandings of maturation, but still they seem like the childhood syndromes in fundamental ways.

Many of the symptoms of the loneliness of emotional isolation seem to stem from a re-experiencing of the anxiety produced by childhood abandonment. This is a central theme, and gives rise to a sense of pervasive apprehensiveness—one of our respondents called it "a nameless fear"[18]—that may prevent concentration on reading or television and almost force the individual into some sort of motor activity as a channel for his or her jumpiness.

Associated with apprehensiveness is sometimes vigilance to threat, a readiness to hear sounds in the night, which keeps one tense, unable to relax enough to sleep. Often though, vigilence seems less to be directed to threat than to possible remedy; the individual is forever appraising others for their potential as providers of the needed relationship, and forever appraising situations in terms of their potential for making the needed relationships available. The lonely individual's perceptual and motivational energies are likely to become organized in the service of finding remedies for his or her loneliness.

Finally, those experiencing the loneliness of emotional isolation are apt to experience a sense of utter aloneness, whether or not the companionship of others is in fact accessible to them. This sense of utter aloneness may be phrased in terms of the absence of anyone else in the environment, in which case the individual may describe the immediately available world as desolate, barren, or devoid of others; or the sense of utter aloneness may be phrased in terms of an empty inner world, in which case the individual may say that he or she feels empty, dead, or hollow.

Occasionally, the hyperalertness of the individual suffering from the loneliness of emotional isolation produces an oversensitivity to minimal cues and a tendency to misinterpret or to exaggerate the hostile or affectionate intent of others. This oversensitivity can make the individual seem to be awkward or foolish.

The dominant symptoms of the loneliness of social isolation are different from these. Feelings of boredom or aimlessness, together with feelings of marginality, seem to be central themes, rather than anxiety and emptiness. Boredom seems to come about as the tasks that make up one's daily routines, because they are inaccessible to the affirmation of others, lose their meaning and begin to be simply busy work. The day's duties then are a burdensome ritual which one can hardly persuade oneself to observe. Again there is restlessness and difficulty in concentration, preventing the individual from becoming engaged in a distraction such as a book or television. And again the individual may feel impelled to leave the home, to move among people, at least to come into the vicinity of sociable warmth. Yet here the individual seems driven not to find that one other person with whom he or she may feel at ease but rather to find the kinds of activities he or she can participate in, the network or group that will accept him or her as a member.

We know less about other loneliness syndromes than we do about the two just described. From the intensity of the desire for an adoptive child displayed by some childless couples (the wife, especially[19]), we might suspect that childlessness too is experienced by some as an uncomfortable driving force, with its own object and very likely its own symptomatology. As we have noted, there undoubtedly are other, although less frequently experienced, types of loneliness as well.

THE PREVALENCE OF LONELINESS

By the "prevalence" of a condition we mean the proportion of the population who experience the condition during a particular period.[20] One problem in estimating the prevalence of loneliness is that loneliness is not a condition like a broken leg, which one has or one doesn't have, but is nearer to fatigue, a condition that can vary from the barely perceptible to the overwhelming. How much loneliness must one feel for it to be counted?

Survey studies leave it to respondents to answer this question. At least two survey studies have been conducted to determine the prevalence of ordinary loneliness, each of which asked respondents whether during a particular time period they had felt "very lonely or remote from other people." Presumably including the phrase "remote from other people" amplified what had been intended by the word "lonely" but did not add to it some foreign syndrome. In any event it was in each case the responsibility of respondents to decide whether they had experienced loneliness or remoteness and, if so, whether the experience had been sufficiently severe to justify the adverb *very*. We might suspect that the more introspective, the more sensitive, and the more candid respondents may have over-reported in comparison with others. We might also suspect that those who considered that a certain amount of loneliness might be normal for their situation—the unmarried or the aged for example—might have under-reported. Nevertheless, these are the only statistics we have, and despite their limitations we must make the best of them.

In the first survey the full question was, "During the past few weeks, did you ever feel very lonely or remote from other people?" Twenty-six percent of a national sample responded that they had. The loneliness clearly had mattered to them: those reporting themselves to have been "very lonely or remote from other people" were likely also to have reported themselves to have been "depressed or very unhappy." [21]

In another survey, one in which a national sample was interviewed by telephone, respondents were asked whether *during the past week* they had ever felt very lonely or remote from other people. Because the time frame was narrower than that in the first survey, and perhaps because telephone interviewing leads to more limited rapport than face-to-face methods, the percentage of respondents answering that they had been very lonely or remote from others dropped to 11 percent[22]—still an appreciable proportion of the population.

In this study women were more likely to report loneliness than men: 14 percent compared with 9 percent. Whether this was because women actually suffered greater loneliness or because it is easier for women to admit to loneliness cannot be known.

Marital status was of even greater importance than sex. Of those who were not married, 27 percent of the women and 23 percent of men reported severe loneliness in the preceding week, whereas among the married the percentages were 10 percent for women and 6 percent for men. Severe loneliness appears to be unusual among married men, somewhat more prevalent among married women, and quite prevalent among the unmarried of both sexes.

One might expect loneliness to be especially prevalent among the widowed and divorced. Over half of the small number (16) of widowed men in the telephone survey reported severe loneliness in the preceding week. The proportion for widowed women was much smaller, though still very high: 29 percent. In another study, however, Lopata found

48 percent of a sample of widows reporting loneliness to be the leading problem in their lives and another 22 percent reporting that loneliness was an issue for them.[23] There were too few cases of presently divorced individuals in the telephone survey to provide reliable figures. But on the basis of a rather impressionistic study of those who had just separated from a spouse, Hunt writes: "Of all the negative feelings of the newly separated, none is more common or more important than loneliness. Only a minority fail to suffer from it, and even those who most keenly desired the end of the marriage often find the initial loneliness excruciating." [24]

It is significant that among the unmarried the percentage of women who were severely lonely is not appreciably greater than the percentage of men. Women on their own sometimes suppose that loneliness is a woman's affliction. They envy what they perceive as the ability of men to get out of the house to theaters or bars or sporting events without having first to arrange for an escort or at least a protective friend. They sometimes wish it was socially permissable for them as well as for men to take the initiative in exploring new ties. But women may exaggerate the worth of the right to make the first move: courtship is a two-person game and the primary problem of courtship, which men share with women, is that of finding a partner with whom to play. Women also tend to overlook the lesser accessibility of same-sex friendships to men past early adulthood: it seems far easier for women in our society to establish close friendships with other women than for men to establish such friendships with other men. It also seems easier for women than for men to keep in touch by telephone or lunches or evening get-togethers with an extended network of not-quite-so-close friends. Kin ties, too, are more often retained in good repair by women than by men.

The telephone survey study also showed that those who were poor were especially likely to be lonely.[25] Why this might be the case can only be surmised, but perhaps with low income there is a tendency to social withdrawal. In addition there may be different social patterns at different income levels, and the patterns maintained by the poor may be more vulnerable to failure. Furthermore, aging may be productive of both poverty and loneliness and so responsible for some of the apparent connection between the last two. In partial corroboration of this surmise, some correlation does exist between loneliness and age and we know from other data that a correlation exists between age and poverty. Ill health may also produce both poverty and loneliness. A fairly strong correlation exists between loneliness and ill health and again we know from other data that ill health and poverty are associated.[26]

The telephone interview study found that if respondents were divided into three age groups, with ages thirty-five and fifty-five being the points of division, little difference in reported loneliness occurred among men in the various age groups, but some difference did occur among women.[27] Those women over age fifty-five were somewhat more likely than other women to report loneliness: more than 16 percent among the older women compared with less than 13 percent among the younger. This slight bulge in the category of older women may result not only from widowhood but also from children having left home, an event that may perhaps produce a form of loneliness distinct from those discussed here.

27 THE STUDY OF LONELINESS

We might suspect that had the telephone survey interviewed an appreciable number of individuals of more than seventy years, much more loneliness would have been found. It seems probable that both men and women who are very old are especially vulnerable to the loss of critically important social ties and, therefore, to loneliness. However we cannot as yet demonstrate this with survey data.[28]

NOTES

1. Harry Stack Sullivan, *The Interpersonal Theory of Psychiatry* (New York: W. W. Norton, 1953), p. 262.

2. Sullivan saw loneliness as uniformly painful. Not all later writers agree. Among those who do are: Frieda Fromm-Reichmann, "Loneliness," *Psychiatry* 22, no. 1 (January 1959): 1; Henry D. Witzleben, "On loneliness," *Psychiatry* 21 (1968): 37–43; Klaus W. Berblinger, "A psychiatrist looks at loneliness," *Psychosomatics* 9, no. 2 (1968): 96–102. Among those who find redeeming features in loneliness, while, also recognizing that it carries potential for pain, are Clark E. Moustakas, *Loneliness* (Englewood Cliffs, N.J.: Prentice-Hall, 1961) and *Loneliness and Love* (Englewood Cliffs, N.J.: Prentice-Hall, 1972).

3. P. Herbert Leiderman, "Loneliness: a psychodynamic interpretation," in *Aspects of Depression,* edited by Edwin S. Shneidman and Magno J. Ortega (Boston: Little, Brown and Co., 1969), p. 155.

4. Fromm-Reichmann, "Loneliness," p. 1.

5. For studies of both grief and dying, see the collection of papers, *Death and Identity* edited by Robert Fulton (New York: John Wiley, 1965). See also in regard to grief, Colin M. Parkes, *Bereavement* (New York: International Universities Press, 1972). And in regard to dying, see Barney G. Glaser and Anselm L. Strauss, *Awareness of Dying* (Chicago: Aldine, 1965).

6. Sullivan, *The Interpersonal Theory,* p. 261.

7. Fromm-Reichmann, "Loneliness," p. 6.

8. Even those who recognize the potential intensity of the distress of loneliness may be condescending to "ordinary loneliness." See for example, Witzleben, "On loneliness."
9. Moustakas, *Loneliness and Love,* p. 22.
10. See Arthur Burton, "On the nature of loneliness," *American Journal of Psychoanalysis* 21 (1961): 34–39.
11. Sullivan, *The Interpersonal Theory,* p. 290.
12. Magno J. Ortega, "Depression, loneliness, and unhappiness," in *Aspects of Depression* edited by Edwin S. Schneidman and Magno J. Ortega (Boston: Little, Brown and Co., 1969), pp. 143–153.
13. Parkes, *Bereavement.* See also James R. Averill, "Grief; its nature and significance," *Psychological Bulletin,* 70, no. 6 (1968): 721–748.
14. *Webster's Third New International Dictionary* (Springfield, Mass.: G. and C. Merriam Company, 1968).
15. For a category system of relational provisions, see Robert S. Weiss, "Fund of sociability," *Trans-actions,* July/August, 1969. For the problems of those away from kin over the Christmas holiday, see Mark Benney, Robert S. Weiss, Rolf Meyersohn, and David Reisman, "Christmas in an apartment-hotel," *American Journal of Sociology* (November 1959): 233–240.
16. See the case studies of Mrs. Graham (section 4) and Mrs. Davis (section 6), this volume, for relevant cases and the last paper in section 6 for the experience of members of Parents Without Partners.
17. See Weiss, "Fund of sociability." Also see the case study of Mrs. Phillips (section 5), this volume.
18. See Mrs. Graham in section 4.
19. H. David Kirk, *Shared Fate: A Theory of Adoption and Mental Health* (New York: Free Press, 1964).
20. Gartly Jaco, *The Social Epidemiology of Mental Disorders* (New York: Russell Sage, 1960), p. 12. To be precise, the definition I offer is of prevalence *rate,* rather than prevalence.
21. Norman Bradburn, *The Structure of Psychological Well-Being* (Chicago: Aldine, 1969), pp. 56–61. The correlation between "very lonely" and "depressed" was .71 for women and .72 for men. See page 60.

THE STUDY OF LONELINESS

22. Based on data provided by Richard Maisel. For study design and other results see Richard Maisel, *Report of the Continuing Audit of Public Attitudes and Concerns* (Harvard Medical School: Laboratory of Community Psychiatry, 1969), mimeographed.

23. Helena Z. Lopata, "Loneliness: forms and components," reprinted in section 4 of this volume. The open style of interviewing used by the Lopata study seems more likely to elicit evidence of loneliness than the pre-categorized questionnaires used by the Bradburn or the Maisel studies. In addition, the time period under consideration in her study was not so limited. These differences in method may account for the greater apparent incidence of loneliness in the Lopata study.

24. Morton Hunt, "Alone, alone, all, all, alone," reprinted in section 4 of this volume.

25. Maisel, *Report*. Correlation of income with loneliness was .15. A correlation of .04 or greater was statistically significant at the .05 level.

26. The correlation between loneliness and health in the Maisel study was —.13.

27. The linear correlation between loneliness and age was small when the sexes were grouped together. There was more loneliness among the very young than among the middle-aged, undoubtedly because of the lesser frequency of marriage in the former category, and still more loneliness among the aged. The relationship of loneliness and age is in fact curvilinear.

28. Some evidence for this surmise that the very old are especially vulnerable to loneliness is offered by Peter Townsend's article, "Isolation and loneliness in the aged," in section 5 of this volume.

2

The Nature of Loneliness

Introduction

Let us for the moment accept that the loneliness of emotional isolation is initiated by the absence of a close emotional attachment and the loneliness of social isolation is initiated by the absence of socially integrative relationships. We still are left with the question of why we should react to these deficit conditions with the syndromes of loneliness. This question concerns what medieval logicians called "the material cause," that is, the aspect of human nature that makes loneliness possible. What is triggered in us by relational deficit? Why does it express itself in the driving discomfort we call loneliness?

In the first paper of this section Bowlby suggests that whatever the mechanisms of loneliness, they must have become part of the human response pattern as a result of their utility for the survival of the species. He argues that it was absolutely essential for the survival of our ancestors that they possess proximity-promoting mechanisms, and that only those who did possess such mechanisms had much chance of having progeny to whom they might pass on their traits.

What might be the general character of proximity-promoting mechanisms? There are only a few possibilities. One would be the induction by proximity of a sense of well-being or pleasure; another would be the induction by distance of distress or discomfort, which would in turn lead to movement to reduce the distance. And a third would be the induction by distance of entreaties broadcast to whoever might be listening, encouraging them to re-establish proximity. We can in fact observe all these mechanisms: the induction of a sense of well-being by proximity can be observed in the obvious security of the loved and accepted; the induction of discomfort by distance can be observed in the driving restlessness of the lonely; and the induction by distance of entreaties to others can be observed in the sometimes almost compulsive need of the lonely to let others know how they feel.

Bowlby proposes that those early members of our species who lacked effective proximity-promoting mechanisms must have been more likely than others to become isolated from their band. As lone creatures possessing neither outstanding strength nor other natural weaponry, they would have been easy prey for the large carnivores of the savannah. This idea would seem to be supported, as Bowlby says, by studies of infrahuman primates in field conditions. And it may also be supported by the penumbra of fear that seems to surround loneliness: hyperalertness when alone may in an earlier age have improved one's chances of staying alive.

Proximity-promoting mechanisms may have played a role in survival for other reasons as well. Children and even adults would be dependent on at least rudimentary social organization to ensure a steady food supply and reasonably adequate shelter, as well as care if ill or injured. Children who met no barriers to wandering off would very likely succumb on their own even without the help of predators. The same might be true, though less quickly and less certainly, of adults.

Recognition of these realities must itself have been a proximity-promoting mechanism, quite apart from the automatic responses built into individuals' emotional organizations. But nature may have pressed for something more reliable than plain good sense. Vulnerability to loneliness, to an intense discomfort if separated from emotionally significant others, might have constituted this more reliable mechanism for preventing a scattering of individuals that would have been dangerous for all.

In the second paper Parkes considers how one proximity-promoting motivational complex, which he names "separation anxiety," displays itself. Although he identifies the complex as a component of grieving, many of its characteristics continue to be displayed in the loneliness that remains after grief has subsided, although in loneliness it is likely to be more diffuse, less focused on regaining a specific lost relationship.

Parkes' anatomy of separation anxiety describes precisely the driving restlessness of loneliness, except that the specific lost individual of Parkes' bereaved is in loneliness replaced by a more generalized other. His close description of the expressions of separation anxiety also suggests how much of the symptomatology of loneliness can be accounted for as proximity-promoting. We can in this way explain as having functional value restlessness and the need to search; the focusing of attention on the problem of forming new attachments to the exclusion of anything else; the readiness to perceive any possibility of new attachment, no matter how subtle the cue; the tendency amounting almost to a compulsion to enter those parts of the environment in which there is some likelihood of finding an appropriate other; and the strong desire to make one's needs known, to express one's loneliness.

We have here the beginnings of an explanation for at least two of the otherwise perplexing observations regarding the behavior of the lonely: their often ridiculed tendency to exaggerate the interest others take in them; and their compulsion to search for new ties that may lead them to explore even the most unlikely possibilities. The first is a consequence of their nearly exclusive focus of attention on the possibility of new attachment, the second of their impulsion to search.

The separation anxiety Parkes describes is by no means the whole of loneliness. As we have already noted, there are likely to be, in addition, a sense of vigilance, feelings of apprehension, and feelings of emptiness or desolation. But impulses to behave in ways that might be proximity-promoting would seem to be central to loneliness.

It is not clear that the mechanisms to which Bowlby and Parkes direct our attention appear in the same form in the loneliness of social isolation and the loneliness of emotional isolation. There seems to be in each the same driving restlessness, the same alertness to possibilities of new relationships. And each can produce intense distress. But it is my impression that there is more urgency in the response to the loneliness of emotional isolation: that the loneliness of emotional isolation may appear all at once rather soon after an attachment ceases to exist, whereas the reaction to social isolation seems to develop strength only slowly as isolation continues.[1]

The qualification that the different forms of loneliness may depend on different mechanisms, though important, should not obscure the main issue, which is that loneliness is a reaction to the absence of significant others based on mechanisms which may once have contributed to the survival of the species and which still are critical to the well-being of individuals. We become lonely because it is in our nature to be lonely when our lives are without certain significant relationships, just as it is in our nature to react to other deficit situations with hunger or with chill.

NOTE

1. See Marc Fried, "Grieving for a lost home," in *The Urban Condition,* edited by Leonard J. Duhl (New York: Basic Books, 1963).

Affectional Bonds:
Their Nature and Origin

John Bowlby

In the fields of psychiatry and psychopathology there are two propositions, first propounded by Freud, that are now widely accepted, especially among those of us who deal with children and their families. The first is that a great many forms of psychiatric disorder can be understood as resulting from the malfunctioning of a person's capacity to make and to maintain affectional bonds with particular others; the second is that the patterns on which a person's affectional bonds are modeled during adult life are determined to a significant degree by events within his family of origin during childhood, notably his relationship to his mother....

It was noticing the link between psychopathic personality development in children and major disruptions in the relationship of child to mother during early life[1] that led me to become interested in the ill effects on personality development of disrupted mother-child bonds, and, in due course, in the nature and development of the bond itself. Many other clinicians and behavioral scientists have also come to see bonding and its vicissitudes as providing a major key to an understand-

Republished with minor abridgment by permission of the author and publishers from *Progress in Mental Health*, edited by Hugh Freeman (London: J & B Churchill, 1969), pp. 319–327.

ing of human nature and the troubles to which it is prone. As a result there has been developing during recent years an empirically based science devoted to the study of affectional bonding in human and subhuman species and the conditions that favor or hinder the development of a healthy capacity for bonding. The result, I believe, is to shed new light on what humans need or, put more modestly, to bring within the realm of science much of our traditional wisdom about human nature.

It is hardly news to announce that at each phase of our lives we tend to make strong bonds to a few other special and particular individuals, that so long as these bonds remain intact we feel secure in our world, or that when bonds are broken, either by involuntary separation or by death, we become anxious and distressed.

It is hardly news, either—certainly not to animal lovers—that the same is true also for many species of bird and mammal; strong and persistent bonds between one individual and another are the rule in very many species; and, moreover, as in man, the first bond and usually the most persistent of all is that between mother and young. Thus affectional bonding is no recent evolutionary development—still less a perquisite of being human; it is built deep into our biological inheritance.

The essential feature of affectional bonding is that bonded partners tend to remain in proximity to one another. Should they for any reason be apart, each will sooner or later seek out the other and so renew proximity. Moreover, any attempt by a third party to separate a bonded pair is strenuously resisted. Not infrequently the stronger of the partners attacks the intruder whilst the weaker flees or perhaps clings to the stronger partner. Obvious examples of that are situations in which an intruder is attempting to remove young from a mother or to detach the female from a bonded heterosexual pair. When that happens both partners fight tenaciously to remain together.

It is common knowledge that affectional bonds and subjective states of strong emotion tend to go together. Indeed, many of the most intense of our human emotions arise during the formation, the maintenance, the disruption, and the renewal of affectional bonds. Thus, in terms of subjective experience, the formation of a bond we describe as falling in love, maintaining a bond as loving someone, and losing a partner as grieving over someone. Similarly, threat of loss at once arouses anxiety, and actual loss gives rise to sorrow; whilst each of these situations, we now know, is likely to arouse anger. Finally, the unchallenged maintenance of a bond is experienced by us as a source of security, and the renewal of a bond, as a source of joy. It is for these reasons that anyone concerned with the psychology and psychopathology of emotion, whether in animals or man, finds himself confronted by problems of affectional bonding: what causes bonds to develop, what they are there for, and especially the conditions that affect the form their development takes.

Until the mid-1950s only one view of the nature and origin of affectional bonds was prevalent, and on this matter, if on few others, psychoanalysts and learning theorists were at one. Bonds between individuals develop, it was held, because an individual discovers that, in order to reduce certain drives, e.g. for food in infancy and for sex in adult life, another human being is necessary. This type of theory postulates two kinds of drive, primary drives and secondary ones, and categorizes food and sex as primary and "dependency" (as the first bonding has unfortunately often been termed) as secondary. As Anna Freud puts it, it is a cupboard love theory of human relations.

Linked to that kind of theorizing, moreover, is another view, also strongly entrenched, namely that fear responses develop solely as a result of learning what sort of things are painful and then learning to avoid them.

In a word, food and sex are what attract us, pain is what repels us; and we learn that human beings are convenient agents for helping us attain the one and avoid the other.

During the past twenty years or so a great deal of evidence has been accumulating that points to a radically different way of looking at all these matters. First, it is now well attested that strong bonds can develop between individuals without any rewards being given of the sort hitherto supposed to be essential. Secondly, it is now known that young creatures show fear and take avoiding action without pain having played any part whatsoever. Thirdly, a study of animals in the wild shows that, if any species is to survive, its members have to be equipped to deal with much else besides nutrition and reproduction or avoiding parts of the environment that have already been experienced as painful: protection from potential predators is a top priority. As Freud frequently insisted, to understand man's instinctive dispositions requires us to turn to biology.

In his famous first studies of imprinting, Lorenz demonstrated beyond doubt that, at least in some species of bird, strong bonds to a mother figure develop during the early days of life without any reference to food and simply through the young being exposed to and becoming familiar with the figure in question.[2] Subsequently, Harlow, in his almost equally famous series of studies found that a young monkey will cling to a dummy that is soft even though it provides no food, and conversely will spend very little time indeed on a dummy that feeds him but is not soft.[3] Young creatures, it seems, are so made that they approach and remain in proximity to any object, provided it has certain visual, auditory, or tactile characteristics; and, what seems even more strange, come quickly to develop a strong preference for whatever particular object of that kind they happen first to become familiar with. In the course of nature the object in question happens nearly always to be the mother. But in the course of experiment, it is shown, the favored object can be, depending on the species, any one of a wide range of possible objects—from a member of another species to a cardboard box, from a television set to a roll of cloth-covered wire. What the infant is disposed to seek, it seems clear, and what makes him content, is simply being close to some object or individual; and what object or individual he comes to prefer being close to—to be attached to—turns partly on such things as movement, sound, and texture and partly on whoever or whatever has already become familiar to him.

Findings such as these have resulted in the recognition of attachment behavior as a distinct class of behavior. The distinctive feature of any behavior so classified is that it results as a rule in proximity being attained or maintained between one individual and another. Whether the behavior is crying, calling, following, clinging, or any other, if it results in proximity it counts as attachment behavior—in the same way that sucking, biting, pecking, and swallowing all lead to food intake and so all count as feeding behavior.

A second distinctive feature of attachment behavior is that it is normally exhibited by a young or subordinate individual towards an older or more dominant one.

Complementary to attachment behavior is the behavior shown by a parent towards young, and which we can call caretaking behavior. Though seen most notably in mothers toward their own offspring, in some species it is seen also in fathers; and indeed in certain circumstances and species it may be shown by any dominant animal towards any subordinate one. Together these two complementary forms of behavior—attachment and caretaking—lead to some of the most frequent and persistent of all forms of affectional bonding. The other frequent and persistent form is, of course, heterosexual bonding; though it should be noted that long-term pair formation occurs in far fewer species of bird and mammal than does the attachment-caretaking bond.

During the course of human life we expect an individual to engage first in attachment and later in heterosexual pair formation and in caretaking behavior and in so doing to make stable affectional bonds with a few others. Because, however, attachment behavior is the first of these forms to develop, it has a special place: for clinical observation (supported by animal experiment) shows that, in ways not yet fully understood, the way that attachment behavior becomes organized during a person's childhood sets a pattern which deeply influences the way that, subsequently, his or her sexual behavior and caretaking behavior become organized. So there are strong grounds for holding that a prior task in understanding the developing human personality and its health and ill health is to gain a better grasp of the nature of attachment behavior.

In humans, attachment behavior is probably at its most striking during the second and third year of life. At that age, young children most of the time prefer to be within sight or sound of a familiar adult, whom I shall call the child's mother figure, or mother for short. Though a young child often makes excursions further afield, he will tend also to return. Moreover, if mother moves a short distance away, he will usually try to follow her and, if she goes too fast, will protest by crying. When mother returns after a short absence, he is likely to greet her with a smile, to approach her, and as likely as not to indicate, by the well-known gesture of raising his arms, that he wishes to be picked up. The ordinary devoted mother is more than familiar with all these sequences and plays her complementary role. As a result mother and child are usually not far from one another.

Were a child to exhibit no behavior other than attachment behavior, he would, of course, remain tied to his mother's apron strings. In fact, however, he does much else; he explores, he plays, and most notably other children attract his attention; they tempt him to approach, to investigate, and to try out what they are good for. This exploration and play, by taking him away from his mother, counterbalance attachment. James Anderson describes watching two-year-olds whilst their mothers sit quietly on a seat in a London park.[4] Slipping free from mother, a two-year-old would typically move away from her in short bursts punctuated by halts. Then, after a more prolonged halt, he would return to her—

usually in faster and longer bursts. Once returned, however, he would proceed again on another foray, only to return once more. It was as though he were tied to his mother by some invisible elastic that stretches so far and then brings him back to base.

Though exploration and attachment lead in opposite directions, they are closely linked. Young children do not explore and play in any circumstances—quite the contrary. They do so only when they are feeling fit and fresh and only too when they know mother, or some familiar mother substitute, is close at hand. Many little experiments with children of one or two years old who are brought to a nicely furnished playroom show the extraordinary difference in behavior that is produced according to whether the mother is present or absent.[5]

In the one case, even though mother does no more than sit quietly reading, a child soon sallies forth to investigate the toys and to play with one that takes his fancy—from time to time glancing up at his mother either to check her presence or to receive from her a signal of encouragement or the reverse. In the other case, with mother absent, a child is apt to become listless and less active or else so distressed that all play ceases. Then his whole concern is to find his missing mother.

What brings contentment and confidence to a child, it seems clear, is assurance that mother will be available whenever she is wanted. The younger the child, of course, the more frequently and urgently is her presence likely to be wanted. As he grows older, frequency and urgency gradually diminish so that, step by step, increasingly long spells away become a matter of course. Nevertheless, and this is a point I want specially to stress, attachment behavior is in no sense confined to the young; in illness or emergency each one of us seeks the comforting presence of those we know and trust—and moreover feel troubled, unhappy, and anxious if for any reason they are not available. So far from its being regressive, as is sometimes suggested, attachment behavior is a normal and healthy part of human nature from the cradle to the grave.

Let us consider then what attachment behavior is likely to be for. How comes it, do we suppose, to form so basic a part of the instinctive equipment of a large array of animal species, from birds to man? What, in technical language, do we suppose the biological function of attachment behavior to be?

To answer questions of this sort about any feature characteristic of a species—be it the structure of a horse's leg, the action of a greyhound's heart or the feeding maneuvers of a hummingbird—we need to know in what way that particular feature contributes to the survival of the species. Or, put another way, what would happen to members of that species in a natural environment were they *not* to be equipped with the biological feature in question? To answer such questions for man we need to think in terms of evolution and of the environment in which man as a species evolved.

Man is a large ground-living primate and, like other species of the sort, has probably always lived, until recent centuries, in small stable bands from a dozen to a hundred or so strong, comprising members of both sexes and all ages. Observation of other such species, for example baboons, shows that each band usually moves as a unit and that the only animals at all likely to be found alone are adult males. Furthermore, when a band moves off it does so in formation.

Females and young tend to be near the center and near also to the mature males; whilst the young males are likely to be around the periphery. By adopting this formation, the band is well placed to withstand attack. When that happens, the young males, acting as scouts, give the alarm and withdraw closer to the center, females hastily gather young and move away from the point of alarm, mature males edge towards it. Thus a marauding predator, hyena or leopard, ever waiting in the wings, is balked of his prey. Should an animal for any reason be isolated from the band, however, the outcome will be very different. Unless it is a strong mature male able to put up a fight, the predator pounces and all is soon over.

To be isolated from your band, therefore, and, especially when young, to be isolated from your particular caretaker is fraught with the greatest danger. Can we wonder then that each animal is equipped with an instinctive disposition to avoid isolation and to maintain proximity? For any animal not so equipped would live but briefly. By contrast animals well endowed in this regard would become parents of, and pass on their characteristics to, the next generation. Protection from predators seems, therefore, more than likely to be the function performed by attachment behavior not only in man but in other species as well.

If this conclusion proves well founded, it is of no mean consequence. For it challenges in a radical way the widespread belief that food and sex are the mainsprings of affectional bonding and of social life. In this different formulation, whilst behaviors mediating nutrition and reproduction are recognized to play a salient part, behaviors mediating protection are given by far the principal role.

To submit this hypothesis to experimental test, whilst very desirable, is far from easy. Nevertheless, there is much evidence that is plainly in keeping with it. For example, attachment behavior is seen most regularly and strongly in individuals who are least able to fend for themselves, notably young creatures, females, especially when caring for young, and any who are sick or handicapped. Furthermore, in individuals of every age and sex, attachment behavior is quickly elicited by situations of alarm. This we know well ourselves; any major alarm quickly brings people together.

Earlier I remarked that in the traditional model of human nature it was supposed that fear responses develop solely as a result of learning what sorts of things are painful and then learning to avoid them. We know now that that is a very misleading picture. Indeed, for a young animal to approach everything until such time as he had got hurt would mean very short lives for most. Nature in fact is far more sensible. During the course of evolution it has come about that young animals especially, but older ones also, are so made that they take alarm at anything unusual or strange, especially if it occurs suddenly.[8] On perceiving such, they pause or withdraw, at least until such time as they are assured that all is well.

It is very evident that young human children are built to this plan. By the end of the first year of life a child has usually become very competent in knowing who and what is familiar and so is quick to detect whatever is unusual and strange. From that he shrinks, especially when his mother is not there. When she is with him, on the other hand, he is apt to take his cue from her. Should her behavior show him that this particular strange event need not be taken seriously, he is likely to gain courage and, instead of retreating from whatever has frightened him, to approach it and explore.

These basic dispositions of animal and human nature—to feel secure with the familiar and to be wary of the strange—are in the main good guides. For whatever is familiar is likely also to be safe, whilst whatever is strange may perhaps be dangerous. Acting in accordance with the principle that it is better to be safe than sorry, we thus tend when alarmed to retreat from the strange and to seek the familiar. By so doing we are in fact minimizing the possibility of danger and maximizing the likelihood of safety.

In a similar way, to avoid isolation and to maintain proximity to a familiar figure is also good strategy, since once again it minimizes the possibility of danger and maximizes safety. This enables us to account for the prevalence of separation anxiety, which, you will remember, Freud always insisted was something quite different from fear of some threat from the outside world. Separation anxiety, it is proposed, is what each one of us experiences whenever our attachment behavior is elicited and we cannot find our mother figure, or whatever person or even institution has come in later years to stand in her place.

You may have noticed that I have avoided the word "dependency." I have done so because I believe its use has led to much confused and mistaken thinking. In the first place to be dependent on someone and to be attached to them are quite distinct things. For example, I am dependent on an airline pilot to bring me down safely but I am not attached to him. Conversely an adult may be very attached to elderly parents but be in no way dependent on them. In the second place, to be dependent is commonly held to be an undesirable condition; certainly in our society a child is early exhorted to become independent. An inverse value, however, is put on attachment. We respect someone who makes strong attachments, and we feel uneasy about someone who remains unattached or detached. Dependency and attachment are, therefore, quite different concepts.

I have also avoided the term "drive" which again, I believe, leads to far more confusion than light. Instead, the behavior I have been describing can be conceived best, I believe, in terms of a set of control systems—systems that are activated by certain conditions, for example, isolation or alarm, that when active mediate one or more of those forms of behavior that I am classifying as attachment behavior, and that are inactivated again when the attachment figure is in sight or grasp. To describe fully what I have in mind would take me far beyond the allotted space. Suffice it to say that the kind of apparatus I am proposing is conceived as analogous to the kinds of apparatus that physiologists believe are responsible for maintaining body temperature at a certain point or blood sugar at a certain level.

A theory of this kind has, I believe, immense advantages over the theories which have hitherto been current. On the one hand, it avoids troublesome concepts such as psychic energy, instinct, and drive; on the other, it aligns our theories with those of evolutionary biology and neurophysiology and, moreover, suggests new approaches to research.

Earlier I remarked that what this viewpoint does is not cast new light on what humans need but to bring more effectively within the realm of scientific understanding some of our traditional wisdom about human nature. As human beings we make affectional bonds with others because, provided we are reared in an ordinary family environment, we grow up to have a strong disposition to do so—just as we have a strong disposition to maintain our body temperature at 98.6 degrees Fahrenheit, a strong disposition to sleep so many hours in the twenty-four, and a strong disposition to eat so much and at certain intervals. What the scientist may be able to do is to understand better what mechanisms lie behind these dispositions and, most important of all, some of the environmental conditions that promote or hinder their healthy development.

I believe there are many practical lessons which, though they do not originate from the new viewpoint, are nonetheless clarified and strengthened by it. The first is the immense importance of sheer familiarity in giving us a sense of security and confidence, and in giving us also a sense of identity. Children brought up in stable families and stable communities in which everyone is familiar may perhaps become rebellious but never become lost souls. Even though they venture to the ends of the earth, moreover, they still know where they belong; the elastic stretches but does not break.

Given a familiar base the strange is not so alarming, whilst a modest dose of novelty adds variety to life. But living in a constantly changing and strange environment without familiar people and base to return to can provide no sense of security nor sense of identity. This is why the small nuclear family, moving with the breadwinner's work and isolated from relatives and friends, is a family at risk.

A second lesson, therefore, is to emphasize once again the

immense value of the extended family. Given family links, most emergencies can be negotiated without either children or adults or grandparents having to be removed to strange places to be cared for by strange people, with all the stress and distress that such moves entail.

It is unfortunate that the modern technological world works against us. Prodigal in the material wealth it yields, it must be recognized that, by its emphasis on mobility and its contempt for the stay-at-home, it is no friend of mental health.

NOTES

1. See John Bowlby, *Forty-four Juvenile Thieves* (London: Bailliere, Tindall & Cox, 1946).

2. K. Z. Lorenz, "Der Kupman in der Umwelt des Vogels, " *J. Orn. Berl.* 83 (1935). English translation in *Instinctive Behavior* (New York: International Universities Press, 1957).

3. H. F. Harlow and M. K. Harlow, "The affectional systems," in *Behaviour of Non-Human Primates,* Vol. 2, edited by Schrier, Harlow and Stollnitz (New York & London: Academic Press, 1945).

4. Personal communication.

5. M. D. S. Ainsworth, S. M. V. Bell, and D. J. Stayton, "Individual differences in strange-situation behaviour of one-year-olds," in *The Origins of Human Social Relations,* edited by H. R. Schaffer (London: Academic Press, 1971).

6. R. A. Hinde, *Animal Behavior* (New York: McGraw Hill, 1966).

Separation Anxiety: An Aspect of the Search for a Lost Object

C. Murray Parkes

Separation anxiety can be defined as the subjective accompaniment of awareness of the danger of loss. Much stress has been laid upon it as a feature of the reaction of young children to separation and the way in which it is handled has been regarded as a major determinant in character formation.

Emphasis has also been placed upon separation anxiety in adult life and few would doubt that it continues to arise whenever temporary separations occur or more lasting separations are anticipated. That it is also a major feature of the reaction to permanent separation or bereavement is less obvious. One might argue that since separation anxiety is a response to the threat of loss it cannot occur once the loss is an established fact. Major losses, however, do not become "established facts" in the eyes of the bereaved for some time after bereavement, and until they do separation anxiety continues to be the predominant affect.

Reprinted with minor abridgment by permission of the author and publisher from *Studies in Anxiety,* Special Publication of the British Journal of Psychiatry, No. 3, edited by M. H. Lader (Ashford, Eng.: Headley Bros., 1969) : 87–92.

The author expresses thanks to Dr. John Bowlby and Dr. Robert Hinde for constructive criticism of the drafts of this paper and Dr. Kenneth Jones for statistical advice. Most of the research was undertaken with the support of a senior fellowship from the Mental Health Research Fund.

Separation anxiety is evident in the yearning or pining for the lost person which is so severe after a major loss and the most characteristic feature of the "pang" of grief. The behaviorial accompaniments of pining are, I believe, crying and searching for the lost object and I shall attempt to show how these appear in the behavior of bereaved adults.

The "urge to recover the lost object" has been described by Bowlby as a principal component of the reaction to loss.[1] The evidence which he cites is largely derived from studies of animals and young children, and, although much of it is anecdotal in form, its consistency and clarity carry weight. The behavior patterns which Bowlby finds in accounts of the separation behavior of several different species and from which he deduces a common urge to recover a lost object are crying, searching, and angry protesting, all of which are directed towards the object. These behavior patterns have evolved and have obvious value in ensuring the survival of the individual and/or the love object. Thus crying and searching help the separated parties to find each other, and protesting, according to Bowlby, punishes all concerned with the loss and makes it less likely that it will occur again.

It is not intended to repeat here the evidence upon which Bowlby bases his theory nor to cite evidence for the occurrence of this behavior in children and animals. There is a need for systematic studies in this area, and current work, such as that of Hinde on the behavior of infant rhesus monkeys separated from their mothers, can be expected to throw further light on the process of grief.

In this paper evidence is drawn from a series of studies of

bereaved human adults which have been carried out in recent years. These studies show that when an adult human being learns of the death of a person to whom he is attached he tends to call for and to search for that person; at the same time his awareness that such a search is useless, reinforced by lifelong restrictions on the expression of "irrational" behavior and the knowledge that fruitless searching is painful, cause him to avoid, deny, and in many ways restrict the expression of the search. The resultant is a compromise, a partial expression of the search which varies in degree from person to person and even, within a single person, over time.

In focusing on searching rather than on crying and protesting as Bowlby does, it is not intended to belittle the importance of these other features. But both crying and protesting are relatively nonspecific phenomena. A bereaved person has many reasons for tears and many causes for anger. It is only when the anger and tears are clearly related to the lost person that they can be regarded as a specific part of grief. Searching, by its very nature, implies the loss or absence of an object; it is thought to be an essential component of grief and central to an understanding of the process.

The data drawn upon come from two studies, which involved 138 bereaved subjects. The principal one was a study of 22 unselected widows under the age of 65 who were interviewed at intervals during their first year of bereavement. The figures quoted in this paper refer to these 22 widows . . . .

Descriptive information will be included from another study in which 21 bereaved psychiatric patients were interviewed and the case notes of another 95 investigated. In all these cases the psychiatric illness had come on within six months of the death of a spouse, parent, child, or sibling. This study has been described in detail elsewhere.[2]

Although we tend to think of searching in terms of motor acts, of movements toward possible locations of the lost object, searching also has perceptual and ideational components. Thus in the normal course of events the motor activity of searching is likely to bring the lost object within the perceptual field. The perceptual apparatus must be prepared to recognize and pay attention to any sign of the object. Signs of the object can only be identified by reference to memories of the object as it was. Searching the external world for signs of the object therefore includes the establishment of an internal perceptual "set" derived from previous experience of the object.

A woman is searching for her missing son. She moves restlessly about the likely parts of the house scanning with her eyes and thinking of the boy; she hears a creak and immediately associates it with the sound of her son's footfall on the stair; she calls out, "John is that you?" The components of this behavior sequence are:

1. Restless movement about and scanning of the environment
2. Thinking intensely about the lost person
3. Developing a perceptual "set" for the person, namely, a disposition to perceive and to pay attention to stimuli that suggest the presence of the person and to ignore those that are not relevant to this aim
4. Directing attention toward those parts of the environment in which the person is likely to be
5. Calling for the lost person

Each of these components is to be found in bereaved men and women. In addition, some grievers are consciously aware of an urge to search.

Evidence for each component as it appeared in the three studies under discussion will now be presented.

Let us consider first *motor hyperactivity*. All save two of the unselected widows studied said they felt restless and fidgety during the first month of bereavement, and none of them felt retarded or anergic. Observations by the interview confirmed this report, and quantitative assessments of hyperactivity at interview averaged over the whole year were found to correlate highly with estimates of general muscle tension.[3] These findings confirm Cobb and Lindemann's quantitative study of bereaved subjects using the Interaction Chronograph technique.[4] Lindemann's account of this feature cannot be bettered. "The activity throughout the day of the severely bereaved person shows remarkable changes. There is no retardation of action and speech; quite to the contrary, there is a rush of speech, especially when talking about the deceased. There is restlessness, inability to sit still, moving about in an aimless fashion, *continually searching* for something to do. There is, however, at the same time, a painful lack of capacity to initiate and maintain normal patterns of activity." (My italics.)[5]

It is my contention that in fact the searching behavior of the bereaved person is not "aimless" at all. It has the specific aim of finding the one who is gone. The bereaved person, however, seldom admits to having so irrational an aim, and his behavior is therefore regarded by others and perhaps even by himself as "aimless." His search for "something to do" is bound to fail because the things which he can do are not, in fact, what he wants at all. What he wants is to find the lost person.

Taken alone restlessness cannot be regarded as convincing evidence of search. There are other factors such as anger which are also likely to give rise to restlessness. In fact quantitative assessments of restlessness correlated more highly with anger than with measures of the other components of searching.

Despite this there was one widow whose motor activity did seem clearly related to the need to look for her husband. She showed a tendency to keep glancing over her right shoulder. She did this, she said, "Because he was always on my right."

Let us turn now to the second feature of searching, *preoccupation with memories of the lost person*. Whilst we have no sure means of knowing the thought content of young children and animals during the period of searching, it seems reasonable to suppose that their thoughts are focused on the lost object and maybe on the events and places associated with the loss. This is certainly the case with adult humans for whom preoccupation with thoughts of the lost person and the events leading up to the loss is the rule.

Nineteen of the 22 unselected widows interviewed were preoccupied with thoughts of their dead husband during the first month of bereavement ("I never stop missing him," said one); and 12 of them still spent much of their time thinking of him a year later.

A clear visual picture of the dead person remained in the minds of most of the widows throughout the year, and widows reported no blurring as preoccupation grew less. This visual image was sometimes so clear that it was spoken of as if it were a perception.

"I can picture him in any given circumstances . . . " said one widow. "I can almost feel his skin and touch his hands." Another said, "I keep seeing his very fair hair and the color of his eyes," and another, "I can always see him, I can see him whenever I want to." "I still see him, quite vividly, coming in the door." "I can see him sitting in the chair."

The amount of preoccupation with thoughts of the dead person assessed at interview and the widow's report of a clear visual picture of her husband were highly correlated.[6] Although there were a few times when widows complained that they were unable to recall the appearance of their spouse, such episodes were transient blocks in recall rather than lasting states of mind. It is postulated that maintaining a clear visual memory of the lost person facilitates the search by making it more likely that the missing person will be located if, in fact, he is to be found somewhere within the field of search.

The third category of evidence is the development of a *perceptual "set" for the lost person*. Clear visual memories are associated with a change in the perceptual "set" such that incoming sensory data are scanned for evidence of the lost object. From time to time ambiguous sensory data will fit the image of the lost object. When this occurs, attention is focused on the data and further evidence sought to confirm the initial impression. Occasionally an ambiguous sensation is misidentified as deriving from the lost person. Nine of the 22 widows described actual illusions of the lost person at some time during the first months of bereavement. These usually involved the misidentification of existing environmental stimuli. One widow thought she heard her husband at the door; another repeatedly heard him cough at night; a third heard him moving about the house; a fourth said, "I think I catch sight of him in his van, but it is the van from down the road." One woke to hear her husband calling her in the night; another repeatedly misidentified men in the street who seemed to resemble her husband; a Nigerian girl said, "Everywhere I looked I saw his picture. Ordinary things would have his face." Another widow thought she heard the door opening and her husband coming in.

A comforting sense of the presence of the lost person was experienced by 15 of the 22 widows. This was often associated with a temporary reduction in restlessness and pining, which seems to indicate that this phenomenon is accompanied by mitigation of searching. Some bereaved subjects actually spoke to or did things for the absent person, whilst others were aware of resisting the impulse. "If I didn't take a strong hold on myself I'd get talking to him," said one. Another often became tearful in bed at night, "I talk to him and I quite expect him to answer me." One is reminded of the so-called "vacuum activities," which have been described in animals in situations where the normal "releasing stimuli" for strongly motivated behavior are absent. For instance, the behavior of the male stickleback, deprived of a mate, carrying out its "courtship dance" in an empty tank, which has been described so clearly by Tinbergen,[7] is reminiscent of the behavior of the mother who got up at night to rock the cradle of her dead baby. It is reasonable to postulate that in such cases there is a sensorimotor "set" which predisposes the individual to seek for and to find something in the environment towards which his behavior can be directed.

Perhaps the most striking illustration of the way in which the search for a lost person can be associated with a sense of the presence of that person was found in a woman of thirty who had been very attached to her dominating mother. When her mother died, her search was consciously directed towards making contact with the departed spirit. At her sister's home she improvised a planchette and "received" messages which she believed came from her mother. At the same time she noticed a Toby jug which resembled her mother. She became convinced that her mother's spirit had entered into this jug and persuaded her sister to give it to her. During the next few weeks she kept the jug in a prominent position at home but became increasingly frightened by it. Against her will, her husband eventually smashed the jug, and she noticed that even the pieces "felt hot," presumably a sign of life. Not long afterwards she was offered a little dog. Her mother had said that if she returned it would be in the form of a dog.

When interviewed by the writer three years after her bereavement, she said of the dog, "She's not like any other animal, she does anything. She'll only go for walks with me and my husband. She seems to eat all the things that mother used to eat. She doesn't like men."

Quantitative assessments of the sense of presence correlated significantly with preoccupation with thoughts of the deceased,[8] clear visual memories of the deceased,[9] and crying at interview.[10]

The fourth category of data which should be considered is

focusing of attention on those parts of the environment which are associated with the lost person.

Half the widows said that they felt drawn toward places or objects which they associated with their dead husband. For example, one widow kept visiting old haunts and planned to go to spiritualist meetings in the hope of making contact with her husband. Spiritualist meetings were attended by several other respondents. Two widows were unable to leave home without experiencing a strong impulse to return there. Two others felt drawn towards the hospital where their husbands had died, and one actually walked into the hospital before realizing that such behavior was pointless. Several felt drawn to the cemetery, and six of the widows returned compulsively to places which they had visited with their husband. As one said, "I walk all around where we used to go." Nineteen widows treasured possessions which they associated with their husband, and four returned repeatedly to these; for instance, one kept searching and gazing at her husband's clothes.

Even when conscious efforts were made to avoid painful reminders of the dead person, there was a sense of conflict as if the bereaved person was pulled two ways. One widow for instance tried sleeping in the back bedroom to get away from her memories, but found she missed her husband so much that she had to go back to the front bedroom to be near him.

Several turned over in their minds the idea of killing themselves in order to join the dead person in an afterlife. One girl aged twelve was admitted to hospital because of serious weight loss after the death of her mother. She had refused to eat and her father said, "You'll become like mother," whereupon she replied, "That's just what I want to do, I want to die and be with Mummy." Suicidal ideas were also expressed by a widow who had seen the face of her husband after death, "He looked so happy in death," she said, "it made me think he was with her [his first wife]."

This brings me to my fifth category of evidence, *calling for the lost person*. "Dwight, where are you, I need you so much," wrote Francis Beck in her *Diary of a Widow*.[11] Crying is, of course, a frequent feature of grief and one which occurred in 16 out of 22 widows when discussing their husbands a month after bereavement. The fact that they cried does not, of course, mean that they were necessarily crying for their husbands. Had they been asked, it is doubtful if many would have acknowledged that a cry needs to have an object at all. On occasion, however, the object toward whom the cry was directed was quite clearly the husband. For instance, faced with the fact that she would never have her husband back again, one widow shouted, "Oh Fred, I do need you" and then burst into tears. A bereaved woman cried out for her dead baby during the night. Another called to her dead sister at night. She went to several spiritualist meetings and dreamed repeatedly that she was searching for her sister but couldn't find her.

Tearfulness was significantly correlated with preoccupation with the memory of the dead person,[12] overall negative affect,[13] and tension.[14] All these features are associated with severe grief and with the focusing of ideation and perception described above. The association seems to suggest that, whatever other factors contributed to cause these widows to cry, an important one was the memory of the lost husband.

We come now to our final category of evidence for the

search hypothesis, *conscious recognition of the urge to search for the lost person*. The adult human being is well aware of the fact that searching for a dead person is irrational, and he will therefore resist the suggestion that this is what he wants to do following a bereavement. Exceptions occur in those who recognize the irrational components of their own behavior, in psychotic patients, and in children who are less bound by reality.

The following statements were made by 4 of the 22 widows interviewed: "I walk around searching for him." "I felt that if I could have come somewhere I could have found him." This widow was tempted to go to a spiritualist seance but decided against it. "I go to the grave . . . but he's not there," said another, "I'm just searching for nothing." "It's as if I was drawn toward him."

Searching for the lost person was also apparent in several bereaved psychiatric patients. An Australian woman lost her adoptive son and her true son in the war. Their deaths were announced within a few weeks of each other. When told of her son's death, she refused to believe him dead and eventually persuaded her husband to bring her from Australia to England in search of him. On arrival in Britain she thought she saw her son coming towards her on the stair; she became very depressed and cried for the first time since her bereavement. Another woman received a report that her son had been killed in action in Belgium. She reacted severely and four years later, when the war was over, persuaded her husband to take her to visit her son's grave to make sure that he was dead. Returning home, she said, "I knew I was leaving him behind forever." Another woman kept going to the bedroom in search of her dead baby. Another went to the street door to look for her husband. She found this kind of behavior so painful that she consciously resisted it: "I think there's no good going to the kitchen, he'll never be back...."

To sum up, each of the components which go to make up searching behavior has been shown to play a part in the reaction to bereavement. Motor restlessness, preoccupation with a clear visual memory of the lost person, direction of attention toward those parts of the environment in which the person is most likely to be found, and calling to him have been found in some or all of the bereaved people studied. In addition, despite the irrationality of such behavior, a number of bereaved persons were consciously aware of the impulse to search.

The studies from which this evidence is derived were not designed to test the "search" hypothesis. If they had been, there are a number of other questions which could have been asked and which might have thrown further light on the problem. For instance, in none of these studies were the respondents asked whether or not they were aware of the need to search. There is a danger, however, that if such an intention had been in the mind of the investigator, he could have phrased his questions in such a way that he would have exerted undue influence on the respondent to give replies which would confirm his expectations.

Much additional evidence could be cited from dreams and from interpretations of behavior which seems to represent displaced searching, but the chain of inference in such cases grows long, and it has been thought preferable to confine attention to the evidence presented above. Implicit in the act of searching is disregard of the permanence of the loss. A greater degree of this is disregard of the very fact that a loss has taken place.

While he is searching, the bereaved person feels and acts as if the lost one is recoverable, although he knows intellectually that this is not so. Similarly, bereaved people may feel and act as if the dead person were still present, even though they know intellectually that this is not so....

If we accept that the urge to search for the lost object is an important part of the psychological reaction to bereavement, and that pining, or separation anxiety, is the subjective component of this, then we must ask ourselves, "What is the function of this behavior?" Freud has spoken of the "signal" function of separation anxiety in alerting the individual to the threat of loss. Searching clearly goes further than this in providing the individual with a repertoire of behavior which maximizes the chances of reunion with the lost object. In the animal and young child who have no means of distinguishing between temporary and permanent loss, the function of searching is obvious. In the human adult, however, who knows, or should know, when a loss is permanent, it can have no such function. Grief is commonly described as the process by which a person detaches himself from a lost object, yet here we have an important component of grief which seems to have the opposite function, the restoration of the object.

We know, however, that even in animals, unrewarded searching does not persist forever. With repeated failure to achieve reunion, the intensity and duration of searching diminish, habituation takes place, the "grief work" is done. It seems that the human adult has the same need to go through the painful business of pining and searching if he is to "unlearn" his attachment to a lost person.

NOTES

1. John Bowlby, "Processes of mourning," *International Journal of Psychoanalysis* 62 (1961): 317.
2. Colin M. Parkes, "Bereavement and mental illness," *British Journal of Medical Psychology* 38 (1965): 1–26.
3. Product-moment correlation coefficient $r = 0.83$, $p < .001$.
4. Stanley Cobb and Erich Lindemann, "Neuropsychiatric observations of the Coconut Grove Fire," *Annals of Surgery* 117 (1943): 814.
5. Erich Lindemann, "The symptomatology and management of acute grief," *American Journal of Psychiatry* 101 (1944): 141.
6. $r = 0.73$ $p < 0.001$.
7. Nicholas Tinbergen, *The Study of Instinct* (Oxford: The Clarendon Press, 1951).
8. $r = .58$, $p < 0.01$.
9. $r = 0.56$, $p < 0.01$.
10. $r = 0.42$, $p < 0.05$.
11. Frances Beck, *The Diary of a Widow* (Boston: Beacon Press, 1965).
12. $r = 0.54$, $p < 0.01$.
13. $r = 0.73$, $p < 0.001$.
14. $r = 0.43$, $p < 0.05$.

3

Who Are the Lonely?

Introduction

The selection presented next is an excerpt from an English report on the segments of the English population whose members are at special risk of loneliness. The categories of individuals it considers include the college-aged and the old; the unmarried, divorced, and widowed; those whose work forces them to travel; those who are removed from their spouses to serve terms of imprisonment, and the spouses as well; and those whose ethnic identification places them apart from their neighbors.

The report was prepared by a "working party"—the American equivalent might be "committee"—organized by the Women's Group on Public Welfare of the British National Council of Social Service. The working party solicited testimony from professionals who had contact with the lonely and also from private citizens who had experienced loneliness within their own lives. On the basis of this extensive investigation they identified certain situations as of special risk.

The working party's focus on situations of loneliness rather than on the kinds of individuals who might be vulnerable to loneliness suggests commitment to a situational theory regarding the causes of loneliness. This is the theory that anyone, regardless of his or her personality, is liable to suffer loneliness in situations that are appropriately defective. The alternative characterological theory might hold that certain individuals because of the way that they deal with or react to typical interpersonal situations are loneliness-prone.

Both situational and characterological theories can call on everyday observation for support. Most individuals, regardless of their personalities, are likely to be lonely when separated from those they love. Yet it does seem the case that some individuals have almost a vocation for loneliness. They appear to be lonely in and out of season, until their friends become convinced that nothing will help.

The situational and characterological theories are not necessarily incompatible. We could, for example, imagine that individuals who are prone to loneliness, although they do not actually strive for it, have adopted life strategies that frequently bring them to loneliness-promoting situations. And we might suppose that their life strategies are themselves expressions of their personalities. For example, an individual who sustained severe losses in childhood and who in consequence has become pessimistic regarding the trustworthiness of any intimate bond might be reluctant to form such bonds. He might choose an occupation like journalism that requires a good deal of travel or one like psychiatry that promises to make available the inner life of others without requiring a reciprocal commitment from him. But these may be occupational choices that are particularly likely to produce situations of loneliness.

We could imagine still other ways in which personalities and situations might interact. For example, most individuals at some point in their lives find themselves in situations at risk, but some have a happy facility for finding common ground with even unlikely strangers, while others seem always to let slip by opportunities for social integration.

We might find on investigation that individuals possess different characterological tolerances for loneliness as well as different likelihoods of incurring it. We might discover that early experience in loneliness, perhaps as a consequence of loss, may foster a character structure that results in paradoxical reactions to loneliness. Some young people who learn to define themselves as outsiders may, though at times envious of the securely rooted, also learn to feel most themselves when they feel marginal and even to cherish the freedom of rootlessness. For them the penalties of loneliness might seem less severe than they do to most: they might feel that loneliness has always been a part of their lives and that they would not be themselves without it.

Yet while the situational and characterological approaches to causation are not incompatible with one another, it is of some importance to which we give primacy. They direct our attention to different issues and lead us to propose different remedies. The situational approach directs our attention to identifying the defects of relationally inadequate social environments and to suggesting modifications of life patterns that might make available a richer social world or, alternatively, supplementations of the existent social environment. The characterological approach, on the other hand, directs our attention to the defects in motivation or skill that leave individuals vulnerable to undesired loneliness and suggests as remedial programs therapy or education.

Of the two approaches, the situational would seem to

have the greater attraction at this point. We have evidence supporting the existence of situational determinants, whereas the existence of characterological determinants is as yet more nearly a plausible conjecture than a demonstrated fact. We can report the proportions of widows and widowers who are lonely and demonstrate that these proportions are significantly greater than the proportions of a nonbereaved population; in this and other ways we can identify the situations of risk. We can make no such demonstration in relation to any personality characteristic. Indeed, we are unable even to suggest with any confidence the dimensions of character that might be relevant to loneliness. We may suspect that early losses give rise to character developments in which vulnerability to loneliness would be unusual, but whether there would be greater or lesser vulnerability, and in just what regard there would be differences from the normal, is as yet unknown.[1]

From a practical standpoint there is another advantage in the situational approach. Difficult as it may be to modify living arrangements, it is far easier to make these modifications than to enter into the complexities of character change with the aim of equipping individuals to deal more adequately with their social surround. In terms of directing our attention to factors that may be both causal and modifiable, the situational approach would seem to have more to offer.

Finally, we might note the implications for blame and fault-finding in the characterological approach. It is easy to see the lonely as out of step, as unwilling to make necessary overtures to others, as lacking in qualities necessary to satisfactory human relations. In this way we blame even as we purport to explain. The lonely themselves may join in and agree that the fault for their distress lies within them. The situational approach would redirect our attention from the lonely as the source of their own distress to the situation they are in and the difficulties they are dealing with. It would seem therapeutically desirable as well as empirically justifiable to be able to point out to the lonely and to those who deal with them the structural characteristics of situations at risk that make for a high probability of loneliness irrespective of the personality characteristics of the individuals involved.

The working party identified two types among social situaations as presenting special risk of loneliness: the first is the situation of the unmarried, in which there is no committed relationship with an intimate other to fend off emotional isolation. The second is the situation of the individual without links to the surrounding community, because of recency of arrival, personal unacceptability, or for still other reasons.

In general, emotional isolation is risked by the individual who is without a committed intimate relationship. It is for this reason a danger implicit in the situation of those who have never married, but it is even more threatening to those who have divorced and those who have been widowed. In the latter two situations there has been a loss of an emotional attachment; those who never were married have had opportunity to develop alternative arrangements, perhaps with parents, perhaps with very close friends. Incidentally it may be significant regarding the working party's presumptions that they consider the unmarried *woman* at risk of loneliness but not the unmarried *man*. Survey data would suggest that loneliness is likely for each, but in our thinking we may continue to draw on the misleading but not yet discarded images of the lonely spinster and the carefree bachelor.

The working party comments in passing on the damage produced by marital separation as a consequence of imprisonment: damage not only to the well-being of the prisoner but also to that of his spouse. Most studies of this sort would consider prisoners as nonpeople, and it is to the credit of the working party that they do not participate in this act of consenual blindness. The prisoner and his spouse each suffer a loss of attachment figure. The same loss, it may be noted, is accepted almost as a matter of course by families in which the husband is forced away on business trips or military service; but in these instances it is possible for those affected to feel that the separation is in some way justifiable. In imprisonment it is simply another aspect of punishment; some prisoners think of it as the worst aspect. And it is shared by the guiltless spouse.

Both for those who are married and for those who are not, moving from one region to another brings with it the risk of both emotional isolation and social isolation. The young person going off to college leaves behind parents who may by that time only fitfully function as attachment figures and also those peers with whom close emotional ties may have existed. The young person also leaves behind the network of friendly relations that may have constituted a community for him.

Young people who attend a college distant from their home risk isolation if they cannot very soon fit into the life of the dormitory or other group housing to which they are assigned and have no other basis—such as skill in dramatics—for developing a congenial social network. Those who leave for jobs in a new community, whether from home or from college, are likely to encounter exactly the same risks, without having access to the potential networks provided by dormitory housing or the other supportive structures made available by a paternalistic college administration.

Geographic mobility is a major determinant of failure of social integration. But even without geographic mobility individuals may find themselves in situations in which social engagement is difficult to maintain. The young wife tied by small children to chores in an isolated home is in such a situation; to a lesser extent so is the young husband apportioning his time among home and work and commuting, with no opportunity to build friendships or maintain neighboring relationships.

Social isolation may also occur as a secondary effect of the change in one's way of life that follows bereavement or marital separation. The loss of one's spouse brings with it a change in routine, in one's concerns, and in one's basis for social participation that may make it difficult for the individual to retain membership in what had been his or her social network. As a result bereavement or marital separation is apt to be followed by a fading of former friendships. Often not all previous friendships are lost, but nevertheless enough are lost so that the individual can no longer participate actively in what had been the individual's community during his or her marriage. In time new networks may be formed that include new friends with whom the new situation is shared as well as old friends from an earlier life. But until this new network forms there is likely to be a period of social isolation.

Advanced age brings the individual into situations that risk both emotional and social isolation. Bereavement becomes more likely. Social isolation is quite likely; the aged live increasingly with the experience that retirement and infirmity and depletion of energy lead to loss of friends. A geographic move to a retirement home may deliver them to quite hopeless isolation.

If the report of the working party does nothing more, it suggests strongly that everyone at some point in his or her life is vulnerable to loneliness. Only those who are secure in a satisfying close emotional tie and who are possessed as well of a satisfying social life may consider themselves relatively immune. And then only for the short run; for we all must recognize the inevitability of loss and change.

NOTE

1. This was written before I learned of the very interesting work of Vello Sermat of York University reported in "Loneliness and interpersonal competence," a paper he presented at the Western Psychological Association meetings, April 1973. He found, in preliminary work, that unwillingness to initiate interaction was significantly related to loneliness for men but not for women. Women appeared more likely to be lonely if they were less capable of managing to maintain intimate ties, and less able to make clear their relational needs. These findings are still tentative but they correspond to our imagery of men as initiators and women as maintainers of intimate ties.

Individuals Most Troubled by Loneliness

The Women's Group on Public Welfare

LONELY STUDENTS

For many students their first term at a university is also their first time away from home for any long period. The closer companionship of life in a residence hall might prevent students from being overcome by the strain imposed on them during the first few weeks of university life....

Rediscovering their identity in an adult world presents a particular problem with some students, and they may find themselves in a situation where they need to withdraw and reconsider the whole direction of their life, its goals and values. This state may be accompanied by feelings of doubt, confusion, and anxiety.

Foreign students, especially those who are married, have additional problems. Usually having to live near their spouse's place of work so that the children can be placed in a nursery school, they are faced with long hours of traveling; or there may be endless crises over caring for the children. ...This state of affairs may lead to isolation from student body and neighbors alike, an isolation made all the greater

Excerpted and republished with the permission of the publishers from *Loneliness: A New Study* (London: National Council of Social Service, 1972), pp. 19–50.

by being in a foreign country. Although there are many organizations providing social clubs for foreign students, these do not entirely compensate for the loss of the natural companionship usually found in university life.

Foreign students live in scattered quarters and often do not feel themselves a part of the immigrant community. Therefore they miss the benefit of the close family ties, which do to a certain extent bolster immigrant children against loneliness during the growing period.

Another kind of loneliness may be experienced by the large number of student nurses from overseas who are employed in institutions such as mental hospitals, situated in spacious grounds and isolated from the local community. Language difficulties may accentuate the sense of isolation, so that many nurses do not know what to do with their time off. Local organizations could do much to help the staff of large hospitals in the same way that they help patients, for example, through leagues of hospital friends, associations for mental health, townswomen's guilds, and women's institutes....

WOMEN ALONE

It is difficult to assess whether the single state is more difficult for women or for men....

For those women who remain single through no choice of their own, there are emotional crises to overcome. Realities have to be faced, and the late thirties are likely to be a bad time, especially in the life of a woman who may have to accept that she may never marry and also that she will never bear children. Some women can come to terms with these facts and determine to make the best of it alone. Others lose self-confidence, cease to care about their appearance, and may grow rigid in their ideas and outlook.

For the older woman, social life can be limited or nonexistent: whether single, widowed, or divorced, she may find herself restricted to an undiluted diet of female society. For those who have been accustomed to a man in their lives, this deprivation can be extremely trying, constantly underlining their feelings of social isolation.

MARRIAGE BREAKDOWN

Perhaps there is no greater loneliness than that suffered when a marriage breaks down, particularly in a situation where the partnership has foundered so far that communications between the two have become impossible.

It was pointed out to the working party that the divorced and widowed are often more lonely than those who have never married. This deeper loneliness could be due not only to the loss of a close companion but also where, having married young, they have never learned to live with or face up to loneliness earlier in life.

THE YOUNG WIFE

A young wife is confronted with a host of new responsibilities. Some will enjoy the opportunities for being creative: building up a home, learning to cook and to budget. But having to make both ends meet, often on a shoestring, can be an alarming experience. It is frequently hard enough to make the housekeeping budget stretch to cover the expenses of daily living without having to find extra money for the endless little things that are needed in a new house or for a new baby. To this is added the responsibility of feeding her husband properly and the need to make a comfortable, attractive home to which he will want to return. When the first baby arrives the young mother has the anxiety of being entirely responsible for this helpless object which is a human life—and for up to twelve hours in every twenty-four she may be alone.

Where a husband is aware of his wife's need to have some outside companionship, it may be possible for him to baby-sit one or two nights a week so that she may follow her own interests. With a wider horizon than the narrow limits a home may offer, the young wife will be better able to provide the support and comfort her husband too may want when he is struggling to make his way in the world.

PRISONERS AND THEIR FAMILIES

Obviously, serving a prison sentence not only isolates the prisoner from society and his family, but it may also have the effect of isolating his wife and family. A wife may be shunned because of her husband's criminal record, or she may react to her situation by cutting off all contact with neighbors. She may move to a new area, exposing both herself and her family to a considerable period of loneliness.

Attempts to keep in contact with her husband are often frustrated by only being able to visit him about once a month. Since men are often imprisoned far from their homes, traveling poses considerable problems, both financial and physical, especially where small children have to be taken along too: ...

PROBLEMS OF RETIREMENT

For some, retirement marks the onset of loneliness because it appears to be the end of a useful working life; for others it is the beginning of a new period of activity with time to enjoy those things that the necessity to earn a living made impossible. But for the man whose work has been his life, the loss of stimulus which the need for work provided and the loss of companionship of work-mates and colleagues can seem irreplaceable. His work is no longer his main topic of conversation; he is cut off from purposeful journeys to his place of work, and at home he finds himself in the way, feeling constantly under his wife's feet. She in turn may resent having to give up the way of life she has made for herself during the years when she has been alone all day. It seems that even as on marriage a girl should try and keep up her own interests, so should the older woman on her husband's retirement. This will be made easier where the husband realizes his wife's need, encouraging and making it possible for her to keep up the interests she has developed during their married life. In the usual course of events the man dies first, and if the wife has given up everything to spend their retirement together, she will have lost the support of friends and contacts who could have helped her through bereavement....

DANGERS OF MOVING AWAY

Retirement is apt to be a time at which people decide to uproot themselves and move to a new district. They may quite understandably feel they should move into a smaller house; they may long to get away from the noise and dirt of the town in which they have been forced to spend all their working lives or, in cases where health is deteriorating, a milder climate may seem tempting. However, the working party felt that people should be warned of the dangers and disadvantages of moving away from a district in which they are known. In the first place, those who have reached retirement age do not make friends so easily, and any friendship newly formed may be somewhat superficial. If one partner dies shortly after moving, the other may be left friendless, in a comparatively strange area, just when the help of neighbors and friends of long standing is most needed. . . .

A new hazard for the elderly is rehousing for slum clearance. This may have two effects: that the elderly are uprooted from the street and house in which they have lived all their lives or that they may find themselves left high and dry in an area due for clearance, their neighbors having been moved away to new homes. They are bereft not only of neighbors but often also of shops and transport. . . .

THE WELL-TO-DO ELDERLY

The working party's attention was drawn to a new problem, which has arisen in the last twenty-five years: the number of elderly people who, in spite of being well-to-do, can still be very isolated. There are many people who think that those with ample means have no problems in this sphere, but this is not true: money is no panacea for loneliness. Their problems may be different, their loneliness may arise from different causes, but it is still very real. Old age with money may be easier and more comfortable, with central heating and all the gadgets and devices of the technological age, but these comforts cannot take the place of the old retainers who were life-long companions and friends of the family as well as servants.

Then for people who have led full lives, with a wide circle of friends and many absorbing interests, loneliness comes when this life collapses round them in old age. Some may also have been deeply involved in the life of the neighborhood through membership on committees and the local council: the inability to keep up such activities cuts them off from the community and makes them feel outsiders. In addition, arthritis and failing sight may deprive them of the accomplishments and interests that previously helped to fill their leisure hours.

Although to people living alone and in penury life in a hotel may appear to be like heaven on earth, in fact those so placed may find themselves beset by difficulties. Hotel staff tend to have a rapid turnover, so that friendly links with residents are rarely established. Moreover, in some holiday resorts hoteliers expect their elderly residents to go elsewhere for three months every summer so that they can fill the place with holiday-makers, at high-season rates, unencumbered by their permanent guests. Because they apparently live in comfort the elderly rich get little sympathy or help and sometimes find that even their so-called friends are only waiting for crumbs from the rich man's table. Whatever the comforts enjoyed, theirs can be a very lonely life.

4

The Loneliness of Emotional Isolation

Introduction

Insofar as the loneliness of emotional isolation represents the subjective response to the absence not so much of a particular other but rather of a generalized attachment figure, it is a state that is probably not experienced until adolescence. Children younger than adolescent age undoubtedly experience separation anxiety in response to the absence of the parent who is their primary attachment figure, but this state lacks loneliness's diffuse driving restlessness, its compulsion to locate an intimate other whose identity may as yet not be known. In separation anxiety pining is much more focused, much more object-fixed.

Virtually everyone must have experienced separation anxiety as a child, just as virtually everyone seems to have experienced loneliness later in life. (Vello Sermat, a Canadian psychologist, reports that in studies of a variety of groups he has never found more than one or two percent reporting that they had never been lonely.[1]) Situations that would be likely to induce separation anxiety seem almost intrinsic to growing up. Virtually everyone must at some point have been delivered by his parents for the space of an afternoon or evening to the care of an aunt, baby-sitter, or neighbor, without being absolutely convinced that his or her parents would return. And virtually everyone must have had the experience of waking in the night to a dark and still house and needing instant reassurance that his or her parents still were there. When children are first entered in school they may well feel themselves abandoned to strangers until the distant future at the end of the day. And then there may be summer camp, where separation anxiety is called homesickness; and perhaps, if the child is unlucky, a hospitalization.

Loneliness proper becomes a possible experience only when, in adolescence, parents are relinquished as attachment figures. Then it is possible for individuals to scan their social worlds for attachment and see only unsatisfactory friendly acquaintances. But it is also possible in adolescence for love affairs to be established and then lost, with grief followed closely by loneliness. Among the somewhat older, marriages may be contracted and then ended, again with intense grief followed by painful loneliness. Among those who remain married, even happily married, there may be brushes with loneliness; involuntary separation, in particular, brought about by job or illness or family duty, may produce just enough exposure to the loneliness of emotional isolation to instruct the married in the emotional significance of their bond.

Actually it is not marriage that is critical in fending off the loneliness of emotional isolation but rather the availability of emotional attachment, of a relationship with another person such that the mere proximity of the other person can promote feelings of security and well-being. There are empty shell marriages, marriages without attachment, that provide no defense against loneliness.[2] Indeed, marriages of this sort may seem to the participants to be the chief cause of their loneliness, since they prevent the formation of genuine attachments.[3] By the same token there are nonmarital relationships that do provide secure attachment.[4] Marriage indicates and perhaps fosters secure attachments, but it is attachment rather than marriage that is the issue.

Clearly the systems providing attachment as well as the nature of attachment feelings change as we mature. The changing nature of the incidents that produce separation anxiety or loneliness can be taken as a guide to the changing character of our attachment needs.

The first signs of attachment behavior toward the mother are displayed by the middle of an infant's first year.[5] At this time the mother's actual physical presence seems to be essential for the infant's security. It has repeatedly been noted that infants at this point exhibit "comfort and relaxation in the mother's presence and . . . disturbance in her absence."[6] There may also be at this time secondary attachments to the father and to siblings which, although they do not seem to reduce the strength of the primary tie, do seem to make more tolerable intervals of separation from the primary figure.[7] But at first, separation anxiety seems to be displayed immediately if there is physical absence of all attachment figures or after a brief period in the absence of the primary attachment figure.

The process of maturation of attachment seems to be marked by increasing tolerance for distance from all attachment figures, primary and secondary, so long as accessibility to them is assured. Young children seem increasingly able to maintain their sense of well-being despite physical separation from attachment figures, so long as they are certain they can rejoin one of them—especially the primary attachment figure

—any time they wish. When uncertain regarding the accessibility of the attachment figure, however, they are likely to exhibit symptoms of abandonment: they become angry, often tearful, and insistent on being rejoined with the figure; in time these first reactions may give way to increasing hopelessness and despair.[8]

As children mature still further they become more confident of the essential accessibility of attachment figures despite temporary ignorance regarding their location. This confidence permits them independence of action. Yet they remain liable to separation anxiety on extended separations from their parents.

Adolescence, as we have noted, leads to extensive reorganization of the affective system of attachment. Unevenly, with many retrogressions, the parents are relinquished as attachment figures in favor of same-sex or opposite sex peers. Sometimes teachers or other apparently knowledgeable or accomplished adults serve as transitional figures between the parents and the eventual peer attachment. Idealized mass media personalities may also function in this way.[9]

But it is also possible in adolescence for there to be intervals in which there is no accessible attachment figure at all: in which the world seems emptied, bereft of possible attachment. The parents no longer serve in this way, and there is no one else. Now it is possible to speak of loneliness as a condition of objectless pining, of pining for a kind of relationship rather than for a particular person.[10]

In adulthood the individual may experience attachment to several different figures. What makes possible attachment in particular cases, and what leads to its fading, we do not know. At some point, however, we might expect the establishment of a relatively lasting attachment, perhaps buttressed by marriage. Loss of attachment in this phase of life might be expected to be followed by adult grief, one component of which is separation anxiety, but including as well recognition of ruined hopes and the experiencing of an unwanted revision of social role. In time, as focus on the particular lost object fades, loneliness may become a dominant element.

Bowlby's discussion of attachment in children[11] together with our observations of attachment behavior in adults[12] offers some reason for suspecting that we have only one system of emotions that organize themselves in relation to attachment figures and that—although secondary attachments may be possible—a primary security-providing attachment elicits the same emotions, very nearly, irrespective of the individual who serves as attachment figure. It would also seem likely that there is persistence in the organization of this system in relation to a particular individual. Though there undoubtedly are great individual differences in the constancy of attachment to particular figures, it would seem that in most cases attachments are relatively lasting. Indeed, figures to whom we have in the past been attached often seem capable of again eliciting attachment feelings.[13] It would also seem that for most individuals attachments are competitive with one another; new attachments seem to be formed only as there is a diminution of attachment to earlier figures, and the development of new attachments reduces the importance of other attachment figures. This is, however, a complex area and though it is one that has been discussed in one way or another through the ages, it has hardly been explored systematically.

Attachment would seem to be one component among many in the syndrome that constitutes love.[14] Descriptions of love make it appear to include a set of relatively independent interpersonal elements, the set itself differing for different individuals and perhaps for different occasions of love for the same individual. In addition to attachment, other components that may be found in the love syndrome are idealization of the other, trust, and identification with the other so great that contributions to the other's well-being are felt to be immediately gratifying to the self. There may well be other components as well, including perhaps seeing the other as completing the self by providing capacities or attributes that one lacks oneself.

Attachment is not dependent on these other components of "love." Partners in a soured marriage may no longer love one another in that they no longer idealize one another nor trust one another nor wish one another well. But despite animosity they are very likely to remain attached, as may become evident to them should they in fact separate. Then they may find to their great surprise that in the absence of the other they become intensely lonely.[15]

Except for the unusual "empty shell" marriage, the marital state tends to fend off the loneliness of emotional isolation irrespective of the extent to which the marriage is satisfying. It is for this reason that the loneliness of emotional isolation seems to be a risk almost peculiar to the not-yet-married and to those whose marriages have ended by death or divorce. It perhaps should be stressed that this does not mean that the married are necessarily happier than the unmarried; only that they are much less likely to be lonely.

In the first paper that follows, Lopata describes the expressions of loneliness among the widowed. For the most part she focuses her attention on the loneliness of emotional isolation. She shows that the imagery associated with this loneliness includes not only missing the particular individual who had been an attachment figure but also missing the existence of any attachment figure. She also notes some of the concomitants of absence of a marriage partner with whom one might divide the tasks of one's daily routine. It is not that the routine becomes thereby less manageable; rather it becomes less engaging. While this sort of alienation from one's tasks is distinct from loneliness in the sense in which the term is used here, for the formerly married it nevertheless accompanies and complicates it.

The death of a spouse not only brings about the loneliness of emotional isolation; it also produces that other form of loneliness, the loneliness of social isolation. The widow must function as a single individual instead of a member of a couple. Her new social role is apt to fit badly into the niches provided by her former social network. Her time schedule, her interests, her resources, even the sort of person she seems to be, all are likely to have changed. Formerly a full member of a network of the married she is likely to have become an oddity, the only single woman. Her own discomfort and also that of her friends may now produce reciprocal withdrawal.

Most of the friendships will be permitted to fade, and although one or two may be maintained the widow is apt to find herself marginal to her former social network.

A small number of widows, Lopata reports, presented themselves as not especially lonely. Some asserted that they had always been self-sufficient, had always prized their time alone. Among those who presented themselves this way there may well have been a few who out of pride or in the hope that saying that it was so would make it so presented a brave front that was at variance with the reality behind. There were very likely other widows who had organized lives in which attachment and social integration were provided by relationships with friends or with nearby kin or who had integrated a new marriage-like relationship or who had in other ways contrived to repair their relational fabric. Nor should we neglect the possibility that some widows simply possessed a special ability to cope with loneliness.

We know very little about what sorts of people are best able to withstand loneliness. Our absence of knowledge is indicated by our ability to offer diametrically opposed hypotheses, each of which has a certain plausibility. On the one hand, we can argue that those who are not afflicted by loneliness are individuals who are distant or cool and so form shallow attachments in the first place or who are armored by compulsivities against the threats of abandonment. On the other hand, we can argue that loneliness holds least terror for the mature and self-trusting who have outgrown their infantile fears and needs. Perhaps there are in fact different sorts of capacities to deal with loneliness, some defensive and some not. But all we can do at this point is speculate; no relevant data are available.

The subjective experience of being alone after one's spouse has died is described in the paper that follows Lopata's. A widower, Mr. Neilson, reviews his present life, comments on his chronic loneliness and his partial disengagement from activities and interests outside the spheres of family and job, and exhibits clearly his pervasive depression. Emotional isolation seems almost to surround Mr. Neilson. It would seem that he has just barely avoided social isolation by morning stops at a neighborhood bar where he can share a beer and desultory conversation with other men in the same boat—men whom he says "have no connection." But while this reduces his loneliness to some degree, dependence on tavern life for social integration raises problems of other sorts.

The divorced, like the widowed, experience the grief of abandonment and the loneliness of a life defective in critical respects, yet for those among the divorced who hoped that the end of an undesired marriage might be the beginning of a better life, these painful feelings are often puzzling. And it is difficult for the divorced to expect that friends can understand feelings that they themselves find paradoxical. Now and again a divorced man or woman will express a kind of rueful envy for the widowed whose grieving and loneliness at least makes sense and who can command the sympathetic understanding of onlookers.

The selection by Hunt in this section makes clear the grief and loneliness so typical among the newly separated. In our own work with individuals who have just left marriages for separation, we frequently hear of individuals who earlier had wanted only freedom but who now engage in more or less conscious attempts to recapture their lost spouse. One man found himself compulsively driving past the house from which he had earlier stormed out; when he did his edginess somehow subsided. A woman found that late in the evening when time hung heavy she might almost against her will call her husband to talk with him about her distress, though she did not want to rejoin him.

Like the widowed, those embarking on marital separation are apt in time to find their former friendship networks becoming less accessible and less desirable. Like Mr. Neilson, they will have to find friends in the same boat. Those who separate from a nonmarital attachment rather than a marriage may have an advantage here. Ending an affair, devastating as this may be in other ways, ordinarily does not require that one change one's social role, with consequent unsettling of friendships.

The last paper of this section presents a report by a woman who ended an affair of rather brief duration. Mrs. Graham, the narrator, was the one who took the initiative in ending the affair. Nevertheless her grief at its loss was deep and genuine, and her subsequent loneliness was severe.

Mrs. Graham, like Mr. Neilson, maintained a good many relationships with others. Mrs. Graham cared for her three children, occasionally visited her mother and sisters who lived nearby, was in almost daily touch with friends, and now and again received a visit from our interviewer. None of these social linkages reduced her loneliness except as they provided her with an activity that temporarily distracted her. Being with kin increased her sense of isolation; their situation was so different and they seemed to understand so little. Her relationship with her children, although it gave her a reason to keep going, did little to lift her depression; sometimes her children seemed more a burden than a source of support. Friends helped to an extent; at least she could talk with them about how she felt. Eventually she began going places with friends, especially places where she might meet someone.

Not long after the end of her affair Mrs. Graham's restlessness had become organized into a need to search for someone new. There was a compulsive element in the searching: she said about it, "Even if you don't want to, you have got to go." Mrs. Graham was young and attractive, and the result of her search was a series of new affairs.

Mrs. Graham's report may raise for us the issue of the association of attachment and sexual accessibility. It would seem reasonable on the basis of what we know of the separability of sexual desire and attachment strivings to assume that the two are organized into distinct systems that can be realized independently. Ordinarily, however, the two systems do seem to organize themselves around the same figure. This may perhaps be an expression of an innate tendency to intermesh the systems, but the relative ease with which social definitions can modify the association of "love" and "sex" makes this seem doubtful. It does seem, however, that the interpersonal arrangements that our society sponsors result in attachment facilitating the integration of a sexual relationship and, conversely, the existence of a sexual relationship facilitating attachment. Social definitions may play a role: at least in this country individuals seem to be insecure with attachments that are not yet certified by sexual contact and also to feel that sexual contact is of dubious legitimacy unless justified by attachment.

At this point we can only speculate regarding the explanation for the common observation that in adults attachment feelings and sexual accessibility tend to be associated. However there is no question but that Mrs. Graham was right when she said that no matter which it is one wants, sooner or later the other comes into it.

NOTES

1. Vello Sermat, "Loneliness and interpersonal competence," paper presented to Western Psychological Association, April 1973.
2. In a series of 49 recently widowed women and 22 recently widowed men, only three or four might arguably have had marriages without attachment and these three or four were by no means clear instances. This study is described in the forthcoming book by Ira O. Glick, Colin M. Parkes, and Robert S. Weiss, *The First Year of Bereavement* (New York: John Wiley).
3. Based on comments made in Seminars for the Separated, a service of the Laboratory of Community Psychiatry at Harvard Medical School for recently separated men and women. This service is more fully described in the forthcoming book by Robert S. Weiss, *Marital Separation* (New York: Basic Books).
4. See, for example, the story of Mrs. Davis in section 6 of this book.
5. John Bowlby, *Attachment* (New York: Basic Books, 1969), pp. 199–204.
6. From a description of attachment in infant monkeys given by Harry F. Harlow, "Development of affection in primates," in *Roots of Behavior*, edited by Eugene L. Bliss (New York: Harper and Brothers, 1962), pp. 157–167.
7. Bowlby, *Attachment*, pp. 304–309.
8. John Bowlby, "Separation anxiety," *International Journal of Psychoanalysis* 61 (1960): 1–25.

9. Bowlby, *Attachment,* pp. 206–207.
10. Harry Stack Sullivan said, "Loneliness, as an experience which has been so terrible that it practically baffles clear recall, is a phenomenon ordinarily encountered in pre-adolescence and afterwards." *The Interpersonal Theory of Psychiatry* (New York: W. W. Norton, 1953), p. 261.
11. Bowlby, *Attachment.*
12. See Note 3.
13. See Note 3.
14. Zick Rubin, "Measurement of romantic love," *Journal of Personality and Social Psychology* 16, no. 2 (1970): 265–273.
15. See Note 3.

Loneliness:
Forms and Components

Helena Znaniecki Lopata

This paper is based upon descriptions of situations of loneliness and of methods used to cope with it by widows fifty years of age or older living within an American metropolitan center....

The emerging social structure of the American family and its pattern of residential settlement make the death of a spouse increasingly disorganizing for the surviving partner. In comparison to familistic groups of rural areas and past centuries, modern urban, and especially middle-class, wives are usually left alone when the husband dies. Most widows are older women whose children have already left home for marriage, bachelor quarters, or residential schools.[1] The extended family has been modified to include only limited and periodic interaction conducted from dispersed headquarters. Emphasis upon the independence of each nuclear family discourages parents from living with their married children. Not only is the older couple living alone at the time of the husband's

Reprinted and abridged with permission of author and publishers from *Social Problems 17,* No. 2 (Fall, 1969): 248–261. The study was made possible by a grant of the Administration on Aging, a Division of the Department of Health, Education, and Welfare (Grant No. AA-4-67-030-01-A1) and the cooperation of Roosevelt University.

death, but the widow, health permitting, remains in that unit, or in a similar one of smaller size, for most of her remaining years of life, which can cover more than a decade.

The decreasing functionality of the extended family and mate selection through love have placed a heavy affective, social, economic, and recreational burden upon the marital unit. Thus, the death of one of the partners cannot help but disorganize a great part of life for the other. American widowhood is made additionally difficult by the fact that this society is becoming increasingly couple-companionate in the also expanding nonwork sphere of action. Single persons, and especially single women, are simply out of place in the system, while they simultaneously lack automatic membership in a close sex-segregated network.[2] Those who never marry build over years their own patterns of companionship and aloneness, but the widow is suddenly removed from a familiar world in which she had a comfortable position. Prior friendships were dependent upon couples doing things together evenings and weekends, and they are made awkward by the removal of one member. Sex-segregated friendship groups, such as the "society of widows" found in Kansas City by Cumming and Henry,[3] are often considered less prestigeful. Many women refuse to restrict their relations to others in the same low-status situation and feel anger and loneliness when excluded from the company of prior associates whose husbands are still living. In addition, women were often socialized to be passive, particularly in past decades, and they lack tools for the development of new social roles and friendship relations.

Thus, widowhood presents for an increasingly large group

of American women a break in the major forms and levels of interaction with an individual central to their role of wife, with people brought into contact with her through the husband, and with former associates in couple-companionate relations. It is not, therefore, surprising that 48 percent of the random sample of widows interviewed in an urban area reported loneliness as the major problem in widowhood and that an additional 22 percent referred to it in conjunction with other problems such as finances....

FORMS OF LONELINESS

Widows who explain that loneliness is a major problem refer to one or a combination of the following forms of this sentiment:

1. A loneliness as a desire to carry on interaction with a particular other who is no longer available. Many, but by no means all, widows feel lonely for their deceased husbands as persons whom they enjoyed, whatever the type of relation between them. They are likely to tell anecdotes pointing up the unique personality of the man they miss. Other expressions of this form of loneliness are more simply stated as, "I miss Tom" or "John would have enjoyed this."

2. When a husband, parent, friend, or adult child dies or is otherwise withdrawn from interaction, the remaining partner may feel that she or he is no longer an object of love. Freud and many other analysts of human sentiments have stressed the importance to an individual of being treated by another person as something worth loving. The sentiment the recipient wants others to feel about him may be one of sexual

desire, of companionate love, of understanding and respect, or a combination of all these. The death of the partner of a significant relation thus removes a major source of this identity as a love object, often leaving no other source.

One widow, asked if she considered remarrying, said, "No," explaining that her husband had been a very kind man....

Here I am so big and fat and sometimes I'd be reading and would look up and he'd be sitting there looking at me—and I'd say, "What are you thinking about?" And he would say, "Oh, I was just thinking how pretty you are."

3. Loneliness can be felt due to the absence of anyone to care for or to be the recipient of love. Being an object of love and having one to pour one's feelings upon can be two separately felt sentiments....

4. A loneliness can be felt for a companionate relation of the depth provided by the deceased, for the sharing of experiences with another human being.

I don't think anyone who hasn't experienced it can understand the void that is left after losing a companion for so many years—all the happy little things that come up and you think, "Oh, I must share that"—and there isn't anyone there to share it with....

5. A feeling of loneliness for the presence of another human being within the dwelling unit is experienced by many widows. The generalized sounds of someone moving around or the need to organize work around another person are often missed by them; the opening of a door can herald a major shift in the day's schedule of a wife.[4] ...

It's very lonely, when the night comes you wish someone would be there. We didn't do much but he used to just be there.

6. A feeling of loneliness as unhappiness over the absence of another person who shares the work load or carries out tasks that the remaining partner cannot or does not wish to do is expressed by several widows. Many wives feel helpless in solving problems or taking care of a home when the husband dies. They interpret this sentiment and the related frustration from trying to get the male chores performed by others as loneliness. Having become dependent upon a man who habitually met certain needs, they feel alone every time they seek replacements.

You get so disgusted when you are alone and you have to do everything yourself, especially when you are not well....

7. Another form of loneliness is experienced as a homesickness for the style of life or some set of activities formerly carried out with the other. Many wives who enjoyed company parties, golf, couple-companionate dinners, and other such events, will not engage in them after the husband dies or are no longer invited to them, since it was the husband's presence that formed the connecting link in the first place.

The loss of my husband is a problem; around the holidays it bothers me most. Because the holidays are the reminders of when the family was all together and now he's not here no more and when we were together it was happiness....

8. Many widows experiencing disengagement from a prior life-style and sets of relations express loneliness as an alienation due to a status drop. Women feel less social status in

widowhood due to a lack of a male escort, because of a loss of reflected status from the positions held by the husband, or as a consequence of being a single woman in a couple-companionated world.

I feel the way, how can I put it in words, second-class citizen. Well, I think just the fact that you don't have an escort when you go places. I think that this is very pronounced and very evident if you go out to dinner. I don't like to go out to dinner alone, so consequently you try to get on the phone and call somebody else up and see if they're in the mood to go. This sets you apart; you see a couple of women. I can remember down in Miami—I hate Miami for that reason—when I was not a widow, you'd see groups of beautifully gowned, elegant looking elderly women, you knew they were all widows. Immediately they were an isolated segment of society, in my mind at that time, and I'm sure that other people look at us the same way....

9. The loss of a basic relation partner, such as a husband, can have repercussions in many interaction scenes with prior associates, which can become compounded into rifts in other social relations, thus increasing loneliness.[5] Widows report many incidents in which they have felt unhappy with people who had been part of a previous life. There are several factors contributing to such relational strain with friends following the death of a husband.

According to many observers of societies sharing a Western culture, loneliness in widowhood is partially a consequence of the deinstitutionalization of the death, mourning, and bereavement sequences.[6] Strain occurs over the form and length of "appropriate" grief reactions and over the behavior the widow expects from people defined as part of the assisting team....

The gradual withering away of social relations during a husband's illness, if it lasts a long time, can leave the widow very lonely after his death. Some women mention that they had not realized how isolated they had become, since the very care of the ill person filled the days and the level of interaction had decreased gradually. The traits of grief as experienced by the widow often result in an awkwardness of interaction, if not in its avoidance by both parties. Emotional outbursts or public crying go against the ethics of a society which still idealizes complete self control.... Death and loneliness anxiety, experienced consciously or camouflaged by a complex of rationalizations, contribute to the withdrawal of former friends from a widow.... The widow often feels that she is a "fifth wheel" or that her very presence makes social interaction awkward. The suspicion that former friends no longer wish to associate with her stops many a widow from carrying out behaviors that could increase the level of the relation.... Some of the younger widows feel that relations have become strained because of jealousy on the part of former couple friends. Hostesses are often reported as favoring male unattached guests but as finding many reasons for not inviting their women friends who are widowed or divorced. Of course, the other situation is also likely. The widow, wishing male companionship and to be considered as sexually and personally desirable, may be interpreting any action of the husband as implying advances and of the wife as based on jealousy. Loneliness as a result of decreased interaction with friends is sometimes a result of the prior dependency of a wife on the husband to take the initiative in arranging contact with others. His death leaves her, unless she or the friends change their behavior, increasing initiating action, unable to maintain the same round of interaction. The inability to maintain a desired level of interation with former friends is often a consequence of other life changes: reduced income, not having a car or not knowing how to drive, having to move to a less conveniently located neighborhood, etc.

10. Loneliness in widowhood is compounded by the inability to make new friends, the lack of skills needed to build new patterns of relations when old ones become broken, strained, or not easily available. Seventy-one percent of the widows feel that "old friends" cannot be replaced no matter how one tries to make new friends.[7] Sixteen percent do not know anyone in their neighborhood and 31 percent belong to no voluntary associations. Although they usually do not define their isolation as due to a lack in their own abilities, women who do re-engage after widowhood indicate this to be a conscious process of developing new lines of connection.

11. The feeling of loneliness may be a composite of any of the previously mentioned forms. A widow may miss her husband, find the burden of maintaining her home alone very heavy, modify her life sufficiently to make difficult contact with former friends, and feel strain in their presence, while lacking skills needed to convert casual or secondary relations into ones of greater intimacy.

SOLUTIONS TO LONELINESS

Not all of the widows feel deeply lonely after the death of their husbands. Some explain this fact as a consequence of their personality.

I was an only child. I've been used to isolation and in fact, I enjoy my own company. I don't mean this egotistically, but I can be very happy with me and a book and something to do. Some people cannot stand themselves, to be alone. I always had to have my own time. My husband soon learned I needed time to be alone, away from him. Even as a child, I took off certain time for myself and time to get caught up with my thinking. So I never felt I had to be with people. I am enjoying my freedom....

Closely knit kinship groups provide insured interaction even in urban centers and prevent many forms of loneliness....

For some widows, the death of the husband brought little change—"He wasn't here much anyway"—or only relief—"It [widowhood] hasn't been a problem at all. My life just went on the same way. It was a relief not to have to worry about his alcoholism." A Greek respondent, whose family married her to a man 20 years her senior, stated suddenly, after some hesitation, "Free ... that's what I am, free."

Many widows mention loneliness sometime during the interview, then explain the techniques they have devised to deal with this problem. Basically, the devices fall into three categories: keeping busy, developing new roles and relations, and focusing life on one social role.

The most frequently given "advice to a new widow" is to "keep busy." Busy work may consist of a simple formula for immediate action or a whole way of life.

I find that the lonesome part of the day is at dusk. I don't have my mail delivered and I usually go out and get my mail or do some shopping at this time—just to get away from the house then. People say they call me up at 6:00 and "you're not home."—I tell them it may be a good time for most people but it isn't a good time to get me because then I feel too lonesome, I just get out. I have a car so I drive around a little. I generally eat dinner late at night.... I have a little TV in the kitchen too so I can eat out there. I think it's kind of lonely to eat alone—that's why I watch TV or read the papers.

Busy work may include, directly or indirectly, other people, or it may be carried out entirely alone.

And if I haven't got anything else to do, I'll make a pie for somebody, one of the neighbors that I hear is going to have company—get busy and do something, no matter what it is—just keep busy. Even if you can't do anything else but sit down and make paper flowers—make them. If you don't know how to do it—then throw them away and make some more. Make cookies, give them away; gee, there's always places where you can take pounds of cookies—orphanages ... Lake Bluff. I often go up there during the wintertime. I'll make cookies, then hope for a good day and take them up there, and those kids love them, you know, and it's wonderful. You come home and you think, "Gee, I did something," you know. The space you're occupying counts for something.

Low, that is, nonimmobilizing, levels of loneliness anxiety can lead to a plan of life designed to ensure both activity and social contact. Such a systematic program is very much a middle- and upper-class phenomenon, typical of women who have had relatively extensive educational background and prior involvement in secondary groups.

On Tuesday, I have my hair done every other week. The Card Club meets on the last Wednesday of every month. And then Thursday in every other week the Circle. Quite often on Sunday I go out to dinner with friends; we eat at different places. And then I go to Little Theater in town. They have five plays during the winter.

It is often hard to distinguish busy work from activity carried out for its own sake. The basic difference seems to be that the former is entered into for the sole purpose of avoiding loneliness rather than for its intrinsic value. It is often engaged in early in widowhood. Later, the activity acquires its own meaning apart from the original intent.

The ability to develop new relations in response to the changes in life brought about by the death of the husband is also contained primarily in the middle and upper classes of American society, and even here it is not shared by all widows. An eighty-four-year-old pastor's wife who moved frequently during the first year of a long widowhood, staying for limited periods of time with each of her seven children, and only recently settling with one son and his wife, explains how she has handled loneliness:

> One thing is—keep associating with people and do not be too choosey about one's friends. I mean sometimes people think that it isn't the person you can care too much for—and so often you can find such marvelous people that don't appeal to one so much at first and they are just the people who need someone to befriend them, and they can be marvelous friends. Even these social activities, one can contribute a little. I think one shouldn't be afraid to be useful, even if one has to give themselves a little push.

Changing the role cluster to focus on a new or newly revitalized social role when that of wife is no longer available is one solution to the problem of loneliness. Many women go to work and find enjoyment in its task and relational features. One widow explained, however, that her prior shift into a focus upon the role of mother to the exclusion of other sets of relations is currently causing great unhappiness. Her sons are now getting married and changing their concern to that of their family of procreation, leaving her feeling literally deserted in a form of secondary widowhood. The role of grandmother provided a way out of loneliness for one widow who even followed her granddaughter to Denver when the latter went away to college. Remarriage is a solution to many forms of loneliness. Most respondents state that they are fearful of remarriage because "My first husband was so good," "No one could love me like my husband," "I am too set in my ways," or because of stories reporting many problems in such relations. However, the flavor of quite a few interviews suggest that such statements may function as rationalizations for not having been able to remarry rather than as declarations opposing such a step.

Most widows prefer living alone to moving into the homes of their married children. This attitude exists in urban centers other than those of the United States, according to studies of aging.[8] The interviewees of this study explain that they want their independence, that each woman should be head of her own house, and that "the generation gap" makes differences in attitudes toward life and particularly toward child-rearing a source of strain. "I think it's hard for people of different ages to live together. She [her daughter] doesn't have the same ideas as I do. . . ." However complex the reasons why older widows do not live with their married children, the fact remains that most of them choose to live alone. These respondents indicate that, although they feel the various forms of loneliness at one time or another, they have learned to live alone, and 45 percent agree with the statement: "I like living alone." Very few are completely desolate.

Those widows who are automatically immersed in a close-knit network of family, neighborhood, and/or friends never go through some of the forms of loneliness and have therefore not been the subject of much discussion in this paper. The widows who have or develop abilities to build new social relations and social roles into a new life-style solve many of the major problems which face others in modern society. These women, most of whom have been socialized and educated into competency in dealing with current reality and urban relations, indicate that loneliness and alienation are not inevitable or irreversible. Having gone through a major disengagement from prior life and social relations, they then use emerging facilities of an individuated self and of the complex society to create new life-styles. They choose to live alone, knowing that they can find all levels of interaction when they wish and having self-confidence in their ability to convert secondary contact into new primary relations when needed. The very lonely are women socialized into passive membership in automatically encompassing groups, who now lack such relations. They are the victims of the gap between traditional ways of socializing societal members, particularly women, and the realities of modern life.

NOTES

1. Helena Z. Lopata, "The life cycle of the social role of housewife," *Sociology and Social Research* 51 (October 1966): 5–22.
2. Helena Z. Lopata, "Social psychological aspects of role involvements," *Sociology and Social Research* 53 (April 1969): 285–299.

3. Elaine Cumming and William E. Henry, *Growing Old* (New York: Basic Books, 1961).

4. Peter Marris, *Widows and Their Families* (London: Routledge and Kegan Paul, Ltd., 1958).

5. Arthur A. Miller, "Reactions of friends to divorce," in *Divorce and After,* edited by Paul J. Bohannan (New York: Doubleday, 1969). Also, Morton Hunt, *The World of the Formerly Married* (New York: McGraw-Hill, 1966).

6. Geoffrey Gorer, *Death, Grief and Mourning* (New York: Doubleday, 1967).

7. Kirson S. Weinberg, "Forms of isolation relative to schizophrenia," *International Journal of Social Psychiatry* (Winter 1967). Weinberg, studying friendships in all age groups, found that they decreased in number with an increase in age when old relations were not easily replaced by new ones.

8. This is one of the conclusions of studies by American, Danish, and English researchers (Ethel Shanas et al., *Old People in Three Industrial Societies* [New York: Atherton Press, 1968].) Rosenmayer and Kockeis call this a wish for "intimacy at a distance." Leopold Rosenmayer and Eva Kockeis, "Propositions for a sociological theory of aging and the family," *International Social Science Journal* 1 (1963).

A Widower: Mr. Neilson

Mr. Neilson's wife was one of the small number of women for whom childbearing proves fatal. She had had five deliveries without incident; in the sixth there were complications and she died. A few days later the baby died as well.

When a husband or wife dies of a slowly developing cancer or of some other long diagnosed disease, the surviving spouse has some sense of a continuity of events leading to the loss. The enormity of the loss is not lessened by its forewarning, but the process by which the loss came about can be grasped, at least fitfully, even if there can be no explanation for the process attacking this person, at this time. When death comes suddenly, without warning, in the midst of what had seemed to be ordinary good health, amidst ordinary unthreatening circumstances, the surviving spouse is bewildered as well as desolate, angry and driven to protest, although there is no one to be angry at. The death can hardly be believed; it is so arbitrary, so absurd. For some time to come the surviving spouse will not trust the reliability of anything.

An interviewer from the study of recovery from bereavement being conducted at the Laboratory for Community Psychiatry spoke with Mr. Neilson about two months after his wife had died. At that time he described for us how he had felt after being called to the hospital and being told there what had happened:

When I come home that morning, I was still a little shocked. I was mad, I was mad. I said, "What the hell, why me? What's the sense of this? Is there a reason? What's the reason behind it? There's no good reason." You can't see it to take a girl, a woman, away that's good and healthy and good to the kids and a good wife and everything. I guess maybe another hour later I started thinking a little different, maybe after talking to someone. Then I changed my opinion of it. But I never thought I'd get over it.

Mr. Neilson was about medium height. He had a pleasant, quiet voice. He had played football when he was younger and now had the look of the ex-athlete about him. Before his wife's death he had been a passionate fan of professional football, but since her death he had not watched any of the games on TV. He worked as a maintenance man for a large research and development firm on their second shift, from four in the afternoon until midnight. By working second shift he could see his children off to school, have the rest of the morning to himself, and be at home when the children returned from school in the early afternoon.

Mr. Neilson's younger unmarried sister had moved in with him about two weeks after his wife died. She would come home about five, after her own workday was over, cook dinner, put the children to bed, and then go to bed herself. She was asleep when Mr. Neilson came home at night.

We talked with Mr. Neilson again about a year after his wife's death. By then he had lost interest in most things outside his immediate sphere. He was no longer interested in football. Nor did he follow politics, although he had at one time known local political figures. His interests now seemed to be restricted to his children, an hour or two of barroom sociability in the mornings, and his work.

My days, I usually go out in the morning and I meet these two or three fellows that I know up the Square there and we have maybe three or four glasses of beer. One guy is a Dartmouth graduate, the other guy is a merchant seaman, but he's retired, and the other fellow is an ex-policeman, and it's very interesting to talk to them, because they're in the same, or somewhat the same, boat. One of them especially is lonesome. But we talk together and kid and then I come home to see the kids and then go do the shopping and then go to work. Then I come home and go to bed. That's about it. That's about all.

The little ones, I try to give them my attention on the weekends because they're in school in the mornings. But the real little one, she isn't in school yet. Sometimes I take her shopping. On the weekends I try to sit around with them as much as possible. Or I try to give them a little recreation, like skating or different things. I try to give them some attention. I've been offered a couple of jobs on days, but with the children, the only hours I can work are four to twelve, and I'm quite content.

The kids are my fun. That's the only way I can look at it. I try to get a little interested in other things, like reading, but I just forget it. I mean I just don't have any push.

Mr. Neilson actually saw a good many people during his day—besides his children he saw his sister, his drinking companions, and the men with whom he worked—yet he felt his life to be bleak and lonely. Nights, when he returned home from work, were especially difficult.

In talking with us Mr. Neilson used the image of emptiness to communicate his sense of emotional isolation. He said that he himself felt empty and also that his house felt empty to him, despite the number of individuals within it. In this way he conveyed his sense of a barren, unpeopled world, both internal and external.

When I come home from work in the nights, like I get home twelve-thirty, I feel empty. I feel, coming home, I feel kind of a funny, funny feeling that I'm going into an empty house. Even though the house is still full with the kids, it's just not the same. You know, even if she was in bed, well, she'd always say, "Good night," or she'd be half awake. I get an empty feeling in the nights, I really do.

Mr. Neilson attempted to keep his spirits up, but now and again his underlying depression would break through. This was especially likely to happen when he returned home from work, when there was no one else around, nowhere to go, and little to distract him. Then, even though his children were being cared for and, in that important respect, things were going well, he recognized the bleakness of his situation.

You know, not a lot of times, but once in a while, once in a while if I come home into the night and sit down, and let's say have a glass of beer and read the paper and think for about a half an hour before I go to bed, I get a little sense of despair. It's not necessary because I know that the kids are well looked after all the time and all this, but it's a lonesome feeling. It don't bother me; I mean it does, I mean I think too much, but that's only every so often, let's say every two or three weeks.

I am quite lonely. At certain times of the night, like late in the night I might be at work and I feel that lonesome feeling. And then when I come home sitting in the kitchen alone, like if my sister is gone to bed, I'll feel a little lonesome about things.

Mr. Neilson's loneliness was colored by continuing grief, continuing mourning for his lost wife. The suddenness of the death undoubtedly contributed to this protracted mourning. But very likely all loneliness initiated by loss retains elements of mourning.

I mean, it's a strange thing, I read an article one time in a magazine, about something like this, and they said after a year or so you start to forget, but I still haven't. She's still on my mind all the time. That's something right there that I can tell you.

The times that most reminded Mr. Neilson of his wife were also his times of most severe loneliness. Christmas, of course, was difficult. So was summer vacation, when Mr. Neilson took his children to visit their maternal grandparents.

The loneliness, well, it's still there. But it's not near as bad as it was, let's say before Christmas. Or like around Christmas, that's when it hurts. Or like in the summer, when we went to her parents like we used to every summer, everywhere I looked was her. I mean she was here, she was there.

Mr. Neilson did not feel emotionally free to find someone new. We know very little about the processes by which a particular attachment figure is relinquished. We do know that there are great individual differences in the persistence of attachment to a particular figure. Some widows and widowers seem to remain married to their deceased spouse for years, perhaps forever; others, though they do not forget their former marriage, nevertheless feel free within a year or less to consider entering another.

I know a man's got to go ahead and lead his own life again. Like my sister said to me, she said, "You know, Pete," she said, "She's not coming back." But right now, it's a strange thing, the possibility of remarriage might do it, but I think that's out as far as I can see. Because every time I see somebody I compare them to her. I mean, I've met a lot of nice girls, a lot of nice people, possibly I could have dated them or something, but I compare them to her and I stop dead.

Even sexual drive wasn't enough to overcome Mr. Neilson's sense that a new involvement would be a betrayal. And there were other fears: of getting involved with the wrong person, of being rejected by the right one. Even though others said, and Mr. Neilson partly believed, that remarriage could be better for the children if not for himself, he could not bring himself to make or to accept the initial gesture of interest.

Lately I find myself, I don't know, looking for female companionship, or somebody to be around. The opportunity for sex has come up sometimes—when you go into these taverns you're bound to come across it—but it had no interest to me, because the kids are in the back of my mind. I don't want to get in any trouble with anybody. I've had the opportunity, but this is the way I look at it: I wouldn't want to get involved with some tramp or something like that, because I still have five children to worry about, that's my big problem.

Five years from now, if fortune strikes me, I might be lucky enough to get a mother for those children. But I would want that just for the children, not sexually wise. Not that they're not getting the best of care, but still they need something a little different. They take advantage of my sister. If I'm not around they'll stay up later than they should or they'll go out of the house without a cap on, which their mother would never allow. Or on a day like it's raining or snowing, they'll try to sneak out without boots if I'm not around. It's just if the kid next door's going to do it, they're going to do it.

With emotional isolation comes diffidence. There is no one to reassure the individual that he is worthy of love. Mr. Neilson seemed to have this sense that things could not work out for him. And, in addition, he may have been reluctant to chance another attachment and another abandonment.

I've been told the best idea is to get married again, but I say, "Who's going to bother with somebody with five kids?" Plus now I've got a tooth out and I haven't got a chance to get in to a dentist to get it fixed. It's an embarrassing thing. And then what are you going to say to somebody if they know you've got five children? And it would have to be somebody that was decent, you know. And when you got five children, you just can't walk out and pick up a nice girl.

I'm getting to be a middle-aged man, forty or thereabouts. And the only people that I meet are the people that I meet at the supermarkets or that I run across in beer joints. Because I don't go to dances. I did have this one nice girl there that I was talking to, a German girl, and she wanted to ask me one time if I was going to take the kids skating, and she said, "I'd love to go skating," you know, something like that. But I never pushed it. I just never bothered going any further with it. Maybe it was the consciousness of the children. I don't know. I just said, "Oh God, she wouldn't bother with me." To tell the truth, I didn't see her since.

One of the characteristics of loneliness is its impelling restlessness. It isn't possible simply to accept it and go about doing other things. Sometimes Mr. Neilson called married friends, but this strategy did not work well. The couples had their own concerns, and their very absence of loneliness increased Mr. Neilson's discomfort.

When I get to feeling lonely on the weekend, like after we put the kids to bed Saturday or Sunday night I'll go out and talk to somebody or I'll go visiting a friend. Like I'll call and say, "Are you going to be home tonight?" And he'll say, "Come on over." But you get over and you might find two couples, and sometimes it's twice as bad. You're a fifth wheel. They are good people, but I talk for a while and maybe play cards or something and then I leave.

It was more helpful to talk to other equally lonely men. The loneliness continued, but at least Mr. Neilson was not so alone in it.

I might go up to the tavern, have a couple of glasses of beer with a couple of guys that are in there, that maybe are in the same boat as myself. I mean they have no connection.

Work, too, was a refuge. Work provided a structure, tasks that required attention, reassurance of worth, a community.

What has kept me going is, well, a few beers plus speaking to people and working. Plus my sister coming, moving in and carrying the load for me. But if I don't have a job to go to, I don't know what I'd do. To me work keeps you healthy. I was never lazy. When I worked in the coal mines I used to enjoy it. That's a strange thing for anybody to say, but a job to me is the people you work with.

The solace of beer, however, was not entirely compatible with the demands of work. This might prove troublesome for Mr. Neilson in the future. He has already been warned.

I have been a little lackadaisical about my work. I went to have a couple of beers in the morning and then later, after I went in, one of the superintendents called me in and said, "You're not drinking too much, are you?" I said, "No, I don't miss time and I never come in drunk or anything like that." I said, "It's part of my life now to get out in the morning just to talk to somebody. It's so lonesome now."

All he told me was, "Just be careful. Just watch it, don't get in any trouble. I just don't want to see you get fouled up."

Mr. Neilson tried to maintain his morale by reminding himself that others, too, have their troubles, and some of them have troubles worse than his. Compared to them, he told himself, he was not bad off. But then again he was forced to recognize that he had sustained a major loss and it would be some time, at best, before he recovered.

The way I look at it, I see so much misery in this world, I mean I hear so many problems. Like this man I speak to every day, I was talking to him for two months, three months, and then one time this fellow that's a Dartmouth graduate, he says, "You know, his wife is blind since fifteen years. So he does all the housework." And I said, "Holy Cripes!" Here's a man, late sixties, and he's doing the shopping for his wife, and he's got to do this and that, and I'm only forty-one, and in good shape all the time. I was better off when my wife was around, but I'm still well off, with my sister and all.

But I guess you never get over it. You never forget. Let's put it this way, if there was a remarriage or something, well you'd get over it, but you never forget. And you will never be yourself again. It takes a lot out of you. I'm not quite the same person I was a year ago or a year and a half ago. Time and age does that, plus the hurt.

Alone, Alone, All, All Alone

Morton M. Hunt

Of all the negative feelings of the newly separated, none is more common or more important than loneliness. Only a minority fail to suffer from it, and even those who most keenly desired the end of the marriage often find the initial loneliness excruciating. The man comes home to his rented room or apartment at dusk and opens the door to his sanctuary. All is still and peaceful in his own little haven; he lights a lamp, puts something on the stove, pours a drink, and sinks down with a magazine in bachelor freedom. But the silence that washes over him is menacing, the air seems sodden and and heavy, he struggles to fill his lungs. He turns the page but does not remember what he has just read, has an absurd feeling that something dreadful is about to happen, and can sit still no longer; he leaps up, turns off the stove, and rushes out to a restaurant, a bar, a movie—any place where he can be near other bodies, other faces, other voices.

The woman gets her children fed, bathed, and bedded, and quiet settles upon her house—quiet that pulses in her ears and is full of foreboding. She watches TV, but there

Extracted from *The World of the Formally Married* by Morton Hunt. Copyright © 1966 by Morton M. Hunt. Used with permission of McGraw-Hill Book Company.

is no one to laugh with or make comments to; she tries to read, but it is curiously comfortless compared to doing so in a room where someone else is reading, too; she plumps up the sofa on which he so often annoyingly sprawled without taking his shoes off, and she is astonished that her eyes fill with tears at the thought. In the bathroom closet at bedtime she comes across some of his old prescriptions, abandoned in his getaway; how long, she wonders, will it be before all traces of his living in this home will be erased? In bed, she delays turning the light off; the darkness is full of nameless fears when one is alone. Finally she does turn it off, but stays on her side of the bed, as if he were still there; the night presses upon her, the house makes mysterious noises that cause her heart to skip, and she waits for something to happen. At last, falling asleep, she rolls over, unconsciously reaches out an arm—and wakes with a start because no one is there....

The newly separated have a variety of ways of reacting to loneliness and dealing with it. A fortunate few are able merely to ignore it; they are the self-sufficient souls for whom the intimacy and interaction of marriage may have proven uncomfortable and overly demanding and who are happier in limited, uncommitted relationships. Such persons find the FM [Formerly Married] state relatively comfortable, even at the beginning, and may be genuinely pleased to be rid of the partner. They savor their solitude, as though it were a fine wine. They can buy what they like, move the furniture around to their taste, visit only the friends they prefer, without opposition or compromise. At night after work, or when the children have fallen asleep, such people enjoy the silence and the freedom to do whatever they please. They can eat two peanut-butter sandwiches for dinner, read in the tub for an hour, go to bed at nine P.M., or at three in the morning, shut the bedroom windows tight or fling them wide open—all just as they choose, without asking anyone's permission.

A very different minority, made up of the severely wounded, treasures loneliness as an unguent and dressing against other contact until the healing has begun. A man in his forties makes a fetish of seclusion, regards his loneliness as "a friend and protector," looks through the peepsight of his apartment door before going out in the morning so as to avoid his neighbors, and avoids all human contact outside of work for months until he feels ready to face people again. A young woman uses her vacation time for three weeks of romantic retreat in a remote cabin by a beach; she wants to drain the cup of loneliness to the dregs and to gain strength by forcing herself to face the worst at once.

For the majority of the newly separated, however, loneliness is a recurring pain from which they frantically seek relief. Many, when they feel themselves sinking, clutch at the telephone as if it were a life preserver; they seize it, and through it grasp at friends or relatives, talking about nothing, something, anything—only to be in touch with someone else. Sometimes, in a desperate moment, they will call in the middle of the night, waking their friends, or will phone someone a thousand miles away and gabble of trivia for half an hour. Others find relief in scribbling long, rambling letters to faraway friends or former lovers; the act of writing the letter, even though there is no immediate response at hand, makes them feel less alone.

Some pamper themselves. Men, as well as women, may spend money on new clothing, lavish care on the body, lie in the sun, buy a jar of caviar and eat it alone at home; these mild analgesics are gifts of self-love, replacing the love formerly received from someone else.

Some use liquor. Instead of their customary drink or two before dinner, they find themselves using three or four and having more during the evening. But alcohol is unreliable: though it often dulls the senses and yields a temporary contentment, it also sometimes unlocks the feelings and releases a maudlin yearning for love; then one unwisely phones dear friends and spills forth confused repetitious plaints, perhaps broken by spells of crying, that embarrass and weary even the most loyal.

Many find that a full regimen of activities is the only way to fend off the bad spells. Women build against loneliness an inflexible routine of shopping and housekeeping, cooking and child care, tennis and dance classes, local politics and volunteer work, dates and community activities. Men do the same with work, sports, evening classes, parties, dates, and professional meetings. Weekends need a particularly well-built bulwark of scheduled events, to keep solitude from seeping in. The novice—especially the supposedly carefree male—learns by dreadful experience not to leave the weekend to chance; it is enough, once, to find himself watching the clock on a rainy Sunday, waiting for the next time to eat, turning on the TV for a while and restlessly turning it off when bored, reading the paper from front to back, and looking to Monday morning as a blessed escape from his own vacuity.

Some people who cannot cope with loneliness in any of these ways rush into full-time relationships almost at once; in fact, they may often delay separation until they have some new person standing by to fill the gap. One might call them "chain lovers"—they never stub out one love until the next is lit. Sometimes the new liaison is a genuine love affair; more often it is a mere act of desperation designed to fend off loneliness at whatever cost.

Of all the resources the novice draws on for help, friends and relatives are the most important; many a newly separated person finds their physical presence the only real antidote to loneliness. The end of the afternoon comes, the light fails, and the novice may find himself unable to face the prospect of the evening alone; he phones friends and chats casually until one of them suggests they get together that evening. But sometimes one cannot wait for such a suggestion: an FM, whether man or woman, will sometimes call a very close friend and say, without pretense, "Can I drop in on you for a while after dinner? I can't stand being alone tonight." And as soon as the date is arranged for hours later, the black mood vanishes; loneliness has no malignant power once the FM knows that after a given amount of time he is due to be with someone.

But there are difficulties involved in turning to friends or relatives for comfort. First of all, they are unsure how to behave. Should they inquire into what has happened and into the FM's feelings or pretend to ignore the whole matter, talking normally and cheerfully about other things instead?

If they have seen his spouse, should they tell him? Not to do so might seem a sign of some guilt on their part, if he later finds out, but to tell him they have seen her may spoil the mood of the evening.

And how much should the newly separated person tell his friends? To tell them a great deal may fascinate them at first but burden them with complicity and all but force them to be on his side (although they may prefer to remain friends of both) or to feel dishonest when they see her later and listen sympathetically to her. Moreover, if he speaks freely, he makes his friends privy to his weakness and failures; later he will resent their knowing, since the exposures make it hard for him to recapture his dignity. No man is a hero to his valet—or to his confidantes.

Yet to tell them nothing or very little is to create a gulf between himself and them. A newly separated man may, for instance, visit old married friends for the first time since the break-up; after the first greetings and mumbled regrets about his situation they wait for him to take the initiative, and meanwhile talk of politics, books, children, and mutual friends, wondering if he will bring up the subject of what went wrong and how he feels these days. But perhaps, though he came for human warmth, he is too proud or too ashamed to let them get that close; he wants to be touched, but his nerve endings will not endure it. When he leaves, they look at each other in disbelief; how could he consider them dear friends and yet not confide, not explain, not make sense of it at all? And though they may not say so, they mean in part: Why did he not *reassure* us—for unless we understand his case and see that it is nothing like ours, how can we be sure that it will not happen to us? But only a minority of novice FMs—perhaps 10 to 20 percent—explain nothing to any of their friends. The large majority do offer some explanations to anywhere from a few to all. Some consider it a painful but necessary duty to let their friends know what happened, but most of them have a great need to discharge their grievances and to be reassured that they are still acceptable.

Indeed, whatever the potential penalties of pouring out one's heart, many of the newly separated cannot do otherwise. A young woman, feeling herself nearly suicidal, begs a married couple to let her come visit with them and spends the whole night, until first dawning, talking it all out; they wisely neither praise nor blame her but simply listen responsively, and finally put her to bed exhausted but saved from immediate danger. A middle-aged man, upon the collapse of his second marriage, finds himself making the rounds of all his friends and explaining the separation in "incriminating detail" to each, because he "had a great need for their absolution." A woman in her thirties relates her whole story in excruciating detail to four close friends because, as she puts it, "Telling everything to a few real confidantes was the nearest thing to psychotherapy, and definitely helped me get better." She is quite right; such confiding can, indeed, be therapeutic. As mere "ventilation," it gives temporary relief from symptoms, and when it takes the form of rationalizing—the building of explanations that save face and reduce one's feelings of guilt—it has even more lasting value.

But though friends can serve as psychotherapeutic agents, the process makes both the FM and the married friends keenly aware that there are differences between them now—a narrow crevasse across which they can leap, but which may soon widen into an impassable chasm. Telling too much widens it the sooner: one man who got through his darkest hours by spilling out all sorts of intimate details and grievances to a few friends hardly sees them any more because "they've drawn away from me as though I were a leper."

But the FM's complaining is not the only thing that repels friends and relatives; the positive or pleasurable components in his mood tend to scandalize and alarm them. They may smile and approve to hear of the FM's delight in his freedom and his exuberant rediscovery of well-being, but inwardly they are affronted and shocked that anyone should enjoy himself at such a time. They could more thoroughly forgive him his trespass against marriage if it brought him no joy; his revealing it to them is an act of sedition, and if there is any flaw in their loyalty to their own marriage, they feel the threat and resist it by secretly disapproving of him.

For these and other reasons the newly separated person loses some of his friends almost at once, some of whom take his spouse's side and some of whom drop both of them. He is gratified by the ones who choose his side or neither but very deeply hurt by those who defect, particularly if the latter were old dear friends. He is seldom aware of the meaning his marital break-up may have had for them. A very attractive woman may have been close and dear to her female friends, as long as she was half of a married couple; as a separated woman, she suddenly becomes threatening to their marriages, and they drop her. A man who has been unfaithful wonders why one of his oldest friends never has the time to see him any more; he has no idea that the friend too was formerly unfaithful, confessed all to his own wife, and cannot now associate with him without arousing new suspicion.

The divided loyalties of some of the FM's friends and the desertion of his cause by certain others, augment and exacerbate the loneliness and isolation he feels as a novice. In time, a gulf of incomprehension and divergent interests will yawn between himself and most of his married friends, even those who unequivocally showed sympathy toward him; if he could see all this clearly in the beginning, it would add greatly to the distress of the novitiate period. Happily, he cannot see it that clearly; and at a time when he is first learning to combat loneliness, it is just as well that he cannot.

After the Breakup: Mrs. Graham

Mrs. Graham had been divorced for three years when we enlisted her in a study of single parents being conducted by the Laboratory of Community Psychiatry. Six months before the first of the interviews excerpted here she had become involved with a married man—the husband of a friend. Just two months before the interview the man had left his wife and taken a room in a house down the street. Both she and the man assumed that he would eventually divorce his wife and marry her. It didn't work out, and the man returned to his wife.

The end of an affair does not require that one assume a new social identity, but in other respects its impact is very similar to that of the end of a marriage. Mrs. Graham experienced the same grief and, after a time, the same loneliness.

Two weeks after the breakup we talked with Mrs. Graham about how it had happened:

I was saying I had thought over that thing with Vinnie real thoroughly and carefully and all the angles. But I overlooked one angle, the possibility that it wouldn't work out. This angle never occurred to me. I don't understand why it didn't, but it never occurred to me.

It wasn't lack of affection between us. It was just a lack of strength from him. I suppose it was inevitable from the beginning, and both of us knew it, but did it anyhow. The feeling is still there, on both sides. But he isn't capable of living under the pressures of his wife, his mother, his family, his mother-in-law, her family, my family. He isn't that strong. I think we both had known it for a long time.

Neither one of us wanted to be the one to say let's call it off. But it was becoming a question of time, of how long he would last without cracking. And I would rather see him go back home than crack up. Because even in my lack of strength, I feel that I'm stronger than him in a lot of ways. And I wouldn't want him to crack up because of me. This I don't think I could take. We discussed this and we talked about it and I felt, as he did, that he had better go back home.

I don't talk to him on the phone any more, and I don't see him any more. I don't think that's fair. He's back home. Try and work it out the best you can. We had good times together; we had fun together, and that's it.

Mrs. Graham felt depressed almost immediately. A week later she was still "feeling pretty awful." She wrote a poem "about the world of sadness," but there was no one to whom she could show it. Nor was there anyone to whom she could talk. She had sleep difficulties, which she tried to manage by busy work in the small hours of the morning. Much of the time she was caught up in an obsessive review of what had happened, of whether she should have permitted the affair to develop in the first place, of whether it could have taken a different course.

For the last two weeks I haven't done anything except make two beds and that's it. I really don't care if the dirt piles up to the ceiling. My parlor windows are a disgrace. I can't notice them during the day, but at night when I put the lights on, I can see how dirty the curtains are. I don't care. I haven't cleaned my house for two weeks. I haven't done anything. I'm living in a world that's not even there.

I was up last night until three. I never stay up that late. But I was very, very blue yesterday. For no reason, just the way I got up. I'm not too happy a soul today, but I just sat there last night, and I decided if I do something with my hands I'll lose myself for several hours. So I got hold of some colored seeds that I have around, a piece of styrofoam, and a cardboard. I had seen this done by a man on television. When it's done it's to hold hors d'oeuvres. I lost myself for four, almost five hours. It's putting each one on individually that takes a long time. You need an eyebrow tweezer to pick them up.

Today I just want to lose myself. I'm very depressed and morbid. I don't know if I'm feeling so bad about the fact that Vinnie and I split up or the fact that I was stupid enough to allow myself an affair which everybody knew about. I don't know what my feelings are. I think constantly, but it doesn't do any good. And I cry easily and that does no good.

Mrs. Graham described herself as lonely. We asked her to tell us what she meant by this, as best she could. She said:

How can I explain it? Your house is so noisy all day long, phones, people, kids, all kinds of action going on and come eight o'clock everybody's in bed, and there's this dead silence. Like the whole world has just come to an end. All of a sudden you get this feeling that you're completely alone, that there is no one else in the world. You look out the windows, you walk back and forth from room to room, you watch television, and you're dead.

The images Mrs. Graham uses are silence, being alone in the world, being dead. Except for the last these suggest an abandoned child, terrified at his isolation. The last image, "you're dead," may be based on an interpretation of death as abandonment by the living.

Mrs. Graham was not alone. She had three children, and they were always with her except when they were in school. But this relationship was different from the security-providing emotional attachment she required. Her children were of great importance for her: they provided her with companionship of a sort, and even more, they provided her with goals, with something to go on for. But the relationship with children did not provide attachment, though she was an attachment figure for *them*. Mrs. Graham remained lonely despite their presence.

Like many others in her situation, Mrs. Graham felt that the companionship of children *should* allay her loneliness. She found it paradoxical and somehow a failing in her that it did not. She wondered, at times, about her commitment to mothering. And yet she was forced to recognize that being a mother did not sustain her. Especially when they had gone to bed and there was nothing more to be done for them, she was overcome by loneliness.

It's that children aren't enough reason to keep going. Sometimes they are, but I don't feel it's strong enough reason. I mean, they're there up to a certain hour, but then what is there? Nothing. They're still there, and you're not completely alone. But you are. Kids are fine, but they're not enough. They don't fill the empty gap all the time. They fill it for a while but that's it. After you're done and the kids are fed and in bed, and their homework's done and things are ready for school, there's nothing. It's empty. There's a hollow feeling, a fear that comes over you.

Mrs. Graham's mother and sister lived nearby, but her contact with them failed to allay her loneliness. Indeed, her experience offers a vivid illustration of the general observation that loneliness can be exacerbated by being among people who don't understand and can't respond sympathetically.

> I went over to my mother's for a while. Nine o'clock, I had to get out of there. I just couldn't sit there any more. I got this feeling of the whole house swarming in and smothering me. I played cards, and I like to play cards, from eight o'clock until nine, and then I had to run. I had to get up and get out right then and there.

There was no one among her kin or friends with whom Mrs. Graham could discuss her grief or her loneliness. At times Mrs. Graham felt there was no one she really wanted to see. Having other people around and being unable to talk to them reinforced her sense of emotional isolation. Only her sister Patricia, who was sympathetic throughout the affair, seemed able to offer some small measure of support.

> For the last four weeks I've kept pretty much to myself. Just a neighbor drops in, and my sister Patricia once in a while. My mother came over a couple of times, and then she told me she didn't feel that I wanted her here. I truthfully don't know whether I do or not. Patricia has been pretty good through this whole thing. I don't think I've seen her that much. Maybe once a week. She'd talk about what the day was that she had, things like that, not much of anything else. If I don't feel like talking, she never asks me anything.

After a few weeks, the character of Mrs. Graham's grief changed in that Vinnie became less prominent in her thoughts. She put him out of her mind, or at least out of her conscious mind, by force of will. She was determined to consider him unavailable and, moreover, undesirable: he was married, back with his family, and that was that. Nevertheless, the striving to regain the lost object, expressed in a compulsion to search, remained.

I feel like I'm searching, and I don't really know what I'm searching for. It's hard to put in words. It's a strange feeling, a feeling that you're completely alone, that there's no one else in the world in your spot. If you look at it from another way, you're not in such a bad spot, but you're completely alone in it, and you don't want this. So you look. You look in the wrong places and the wrong things, but you look anyhow. It doesn't stop you from looking.

This restless search without clear object suggests the way grief may modulate into loneliness. No longer is it a particular figure to whom the individual wants to be rejoined. It is anyone, so long as there is the same emotional attachment: in Mrs. Graham's words, "a deep thing just for you."

You look for something for yourself, other than your family, other than your children, other than your surroundings. This is a deep thing just for you. Not for anybody else, just for you.

The restlessness can be powerful. Mrs. Graham compared the compulsion to go out to an alcoholic's desire for drink.

I'll say one thing. After you have been out of the world of the living for several years and you get back into it, you are not going to go back to the world of the unliving again. To the world of seclusion and living for your kids and that's it. You want to slip back into it, but you really don't want to.

You want a feeling of being alive, not that you are half dead. You want to get out. And if you get the opportunity, you go. It's like an alcoholic sitting there looking at a bottle, dying for it to be opened, but he doesn't want to open it.

The pressure to search is relieved when an attachment is formed. But attachments that develop in response to great need are likely to carry a large risk, which may at first be overlooked. Nevertheless, as long as they last, they are fulfilling.

You look for something to fill that emptiness. You start going out. You go with the girls meeting people. Wrong people, right people, it doesn't make any difference. You start dating. Just to get out. Then all of a sudden you wake up one day and find yourself in the middle of something. Then you stop and look and see what you've done. But you don't give up until then, you just do it. Because it's something new in your life. It's something that's filling an emptiness. It may not be the best thing, but it's still something to look forward to, to get up every day for, to dress up for, to comb your hair for, to get a little happiness out of.

Sexual accessibility and attachment seem to be associated with one another in our minds and perhaps in our makeup. If a couple establishes that they are attached to one another, then mutual sexual accessibility is likely to seem appropriate to them and may even seem utterly essential. Conversely, if there is sexual accessibility, attachment seems likely to follow if there is no existing attachment to prevent it.

Couples may use the association of attachment and sexual accessibility to manipulate the development of their relationship. One or the other may seek sexual involvement, hoping it will lead to a more intense attachment, or, alternatively, feign attachment in order to further the possibility of sexual involvement. In any event, as Mrs. Graham notes, both sex and "involvement" inevitably come into it.

AFTER THE BREAKUP: MRS. GRAHAM

It doesn't necessarily have to be an affair, but an affair eventually pops into it. It always does. And it's not necessarily the man who wants the affair. I think women in the predicament that I'm in encourage it more than men. Because they have missed the sexual contact. And if they do find somebody that is compatible to them, then it gets worse. Because you become involved.

The problem of unwise attachments is that they end. One never becomes accustomed to their ending, just as one never becomes accustomed to physical pain or to moral humiliation. Perhaps after a time one sustains less shock and develops better ways of dealing with the hurt. Or, alternatively, after repeated attack one's defenses may begin to give way. Yet even though one knows that another abandonment is a possible outcome of every new attachment, it is extremely difficult to give up searching.

You get involved. And each time you get involved you get hurt again. But you don't stop looking. You just continue looking.

5

The Loneliness of
Social Isolation

Introduction

We have already noted that social isolation may be a secondary consequence of a loss that leads to emotional isolation. The ending of marriage often not only brings with it emotional isolation but also leads to a change in social role which disrupts relationships with friends. It then is likely to be the case that until the now unmarried individual forms new friendships, he or she may be without access to a meaningful social network.

Any severe disruption of social role, through work loss as well as marital loss, would seem capable of producing social isolation. Residence in an unaccepting community, or a move to a new community, may also produce the condition. Indeed anything that leads to loss of contact with those who share one's concerns may give rise to it. We might expect, therefore, to find it among the recently divorced and recently bereaved, among the recently unemployed, among those who move to a new region of the country or even a new neighborhood in a metropolis, among women who have quarreled with neighbors, among those whose beliefs or behaviors conflict with the values of those they meet, among those who are socially stigmatized because of handicaps or because of ligious or racial membership, and among the aged whose networks of association have suffered the combined onslaughts of retirement, disability, and death.

Engagement with peers is nearly as important for well-being, if not actually just as important, as attachment. It is first displayed somewhat later in the child's life than is attachment but thereafter its protracted absence gives rise to almost as great distress as does absence of attachment.

Engagement with peers seems to begin in the parallel play of children between the ages of one and two. It then continues through the games and friendships and neighborhood bands of the pre-adolescent child.[1] The world of peers seems always to be the arena in which the leading concerns of the child are expressed and developed, and in which many of the excitements of the child's life are developed. It is there that children find the fun and excitement of games and gossip, and the social development that accompanies intense and creative discussion of such awesome issues as the nature of monsters or the sources of babies.

In adolescence social participation becomes even more critical to development: the group of friends makes possible expression of the unique concerns of the adolescent and permits each adolescent to feel that no matter how different his or her feelings and outlook are from those of his or her parents, they are valid.[2]

Distress at social isolation, at being "left out," appears very early and is increasingly painful. The latency child without others with whom to play may only wistfully watch from the sidelines or morosely complain to adults, but as the child becomes older and enters adolescence, the issue of acceptance attains almost overwhelming importance.

Sullivan thought that most of us at some point in our early lives had experienced the pain of apparently intentional exclusion: "[An] exceedingly bitter experience with... compeers to which the term 'fear of ostracism' might be justifiably applied—the fear of being accepted by no one of those whom one must have as models for learning how to be human."[3]

The adolescent achieves self-definition in part by identifying with those other adolescents with whom he or she has something in common; in part by occupying a unique place in the group. Self-definition is achieved, paradoxically, by group membership. Continued interaction that communicates a group's perceptions of one may thereafter be necessary to sustain one's identity. This may explain the difficulty sometimes encountered by those who move into a radically different milieu: by a woman, for example, trained in classics or science who becomes a suburban housewife and discovers that the other women in her neighborhood talk only about babies and Babo.

Ordinarily adult men and women seem to find social integration in different ways. Men seem to depend more on the community of those with whom they work and to organize their identities in part to embrace their special work competencies or, among those who have no special skills, their ability to hold down a job. Women seem more dependent on their roles as friends, kin, and neighbors to provide support for their sense of self. Perhaps this difference is merely a consequence of current social arrangements and will change as women are more fully integrated into the world of work. But at least at present when couples move from one region to another the wives, but not the husbands, seem likely to experience social isolation. The men rather quickly find a community at their office or plant which furnishes them with adequate social engagement, although their standing within it may not immediately be secure. Their wives, in contrast, are likely for a time to be without membership in a congenial network of other women.

The provisions of social integration are distinct from those of attachment in that neither can be substituted for the other. The small boy whose sniffles lead to his being kept in by his mother while the other boys are out sledding or, even worse, who is told by older boys to go home and not bother them, will not find the presence of a maternal attachment figure enough to sustain his feelings of well-being. Nor can children be solaced for the protracted absence of parents by the attention of age mates.[4] Children need both friends to play with and parents to care for them. Similarly, adults need both a social network to provide engagement and an attachment figure to provide security.

We earlier noted that the symptoms of the loneliness of social isolation in some ways resemble those of the loneliness of emotional isolation and in other ways differ from them. Each form of loneliness is marked by restless depression and amorphous, unfocused dissatisfaction. But anxiety and apprehension dominate the loneliness of emotional isolation, while boredom together with feelings of exclusion would seem to dominate the loneliness of social isolation.

The prominance of boredom in the loneliness of social isolation suggests strongly that we require participation in a community of our fellows to maintain our investments in our tasks. Even tasks that are carried on away from such a community may derive their meaning from it: a housewife, for example, may think as she cleans, "Now if they come into this house it won't be dirty"; or a salesman as he makes a a call may fleetingly imagine later describing it to his sales manager or to other salesmen. Very unusual individuals may be able to function in response to the concerns of imagined or anticipated communities,[5] but most of us see as meaningful only those tasks that will help establish us as valid participants in networks available to us right here and now.

The importance of shared concerns for structuring individual attention and motivation is one of the reasons for fads. Individual interests and commitments may develop jointly but even if they do not they are likely to develop along similar lines because of the prior development of shared values and frames of reference. As a result it may happen that in a social network one family at a time may decide to buy land in the country and build a summer home there until eventually the decision has been made by almost all the families in the network, without any of them feeling especially influenced by the actions of others. In other social networks there may be a rash of identical serious or trival developments of commitments and concerns as a result of similar processes; there may be a sudden rash of marriages or divorces or new babies or passions for bridge or parties or concern for neighborhood improvement.

Integration into social networks provides individuals with much more than simple support for particular structurings of reality. It also provides them with information, advice, evaluation of their own behaviors and those of others, and occasional help through the device of favor exchange.

Without these multiple supportive provisions of social integration, daily life would be more difficult. The socially isolated have no one to consult about the merits of one or another grocery or film or pediatrician or from whom to learn about current developments in that sector of reality that immediately affects them. In consequence, they are less able to deal effectively with their world. They are likely to have failed to learn that there is a dog down the street that has already bitten a neighborhood child or that the local school has a mixed reputation. They have no one to turn to when they need advice on which contractor or oil company to engage or on how to deal with a school teacher. In these circumstances they may be more likely than the better integrated person to make unwise decisions, decisions that would have been slowed had they been able to discuss them with others. And when they act on their decisions they cannot count on the support of friends or neighbors.

We should not omit from this review of the provisions of social integration the simple pleasures of sociability. Social networks provide a base for social activities, for outings and parties and get-togethers with people with whom one has much in common; they provide a pool of others among whom one can find companions for an evening's conversation or for some portion of the daily round. Social isolation removes these gratifications; it very directly impoverishes life.

Weissman and Paykel, in the first article of this section, discuss the impact of geographical mobility on well-being. Much of the distress they describe either stems from social isolation or is complicated by social isolation.

It is interesting how some of the criticisms once made of life in the suburbs, which now have been shown to have been exaggerated, are given a more precise statement by Weissman and Paykel. The suburbs are oppressive primarily to those women who are outside its friendship and neighboring networks. They are oppressive not because of the suburb's deadly sameness or because the women in them are marooned once the men leave for work but rather because the low population density of the suburbs, together with their geographical isolation, means that the woman who is a newcomer, or the woman whose interests are different, has less chance to find a network that will accept her than she does in the city. Those women who are not accepted by the few available social networks or whose concerns cannot be shared with them are simply stuck.

In the case of Mrs. Phillips, which follows the Weissman and Paykel article, a woman who had the misfortune to be a newcomer into an uncongenial suburb describes her experience. Her marriage, in many ways an excellent one, began to suffer from her pervasive dissatisfaction. Isolated in the new community, she listened hungrily to her husband's stories of meeting people during his work day and then was furious with envy. She was bored and miserable. Finally she and her husband moved into a suburb in which there were people they felt to be like themselves, where she could make a place for herself. Almost instantly her symptoms vanished.

We sometimes think that moving into old age is something like moving into a new region of the community, a less sociable one in which the residents are content each to retire into his own room. Some have believed that a sort of disengagement was natural to aging, an analogue to retirement from work in the sphere of relationships with kin and friends and others. This disengagement theory supposes that the aged accept, if they do not actually welcome, whatever loneliness comes their way, that they have learned to tolerate, and perhaps even desire, isolation. Townsend, in the last paper in this section, suggests that this is not so. He shows that loneliness can be deep and painful throughout life and indeed seems all the more frequent among those who have reached more advanced ages.

Townsend found within his sample of the aged that it was not so much how many relationships one had nor how frequently one made contact within these relationships that determined whether or not one was lonely, but whether one maintained the relationships that were essential to one's well-being. This is not quite his interpretation of his data, but I think his data support it. Loneliness was associated with isolation, to be sure, but was most marked among those who had recently—within the previous five years or so—sustained losses of essential ties, whether they had other ties or not. A problem is posed to our theory by those who had lost essential relationships more than five years before the time of the interview who were not suffering from loneliness. Perhaps they had formed substitute relationships; perhaps they had somehow learned to accept and to minimize their loneliness; perhaps they had sunk into emotional apathy. This last group aside, Townsend's material effectively demonstrates that aging does not end our need for others and that one of the risks of the aging process is the loss of those others on whom our well-being depends.

NOTES

1. Ronald C. Johnson and Jean R. Medinus, *Child Psychology: Behavior and Development* (New York: John Wiley, 1965), pp. 317–319.
2. See the excellent chapter on friendship in Elizabeth Douvan and Joseph Adelson, *The Adolescent Experience* (New York: John Wiley, 1966), pp. 174–228.
3. Harry Stack Sullivan, *The Interpersonal Theory of Psychiatry* (New York: W. W. Norton, 1953), p. 261.
4. In exceptional circumstances individuals may rely on close-knit groups in which they have membership for provisions very much like those of attachment figures. This was shown to be the case for a small group of three-year-olds whose parents had been lost in the concentration camps. The children had received adequate physical care but had had only one another to rely on emotionally. See Anna Freud and Sophie Dann, "An experiment in group upbringing," *The Psychoanalytic Study of the Child*, Vol. 6 (1951), pp. 127–168.
5. Erik H. Erikson refers to George Bernard Shaw's sustaining himself in his early life through imagined membership in the company of great writers. See Erik H. Erikson, *Identity and the Life Cycle*, published as *Psychological Issues* Monograph #1 (New York: International Universities Press, 1959), pp. 104–107.

Moving and Depression in Women

Myrna M. Weissman and Eugene S. Paykel

It is generally believed that most Americans have adapted to the geographical mobility of contemporary life with relative ease and little anxiety. Unfortunately, reality does not coincide with expectation—in fact, moves quite often generate a great deal of stress. But social pressures inhibit personal acceptance of this stress, and difficulties in coping with the problems of moving come to be regarded as personal inadequacies and failures. And while moving can be beneficial, it can also mean multiple losses to the individual—loss of important social ties, familiar living patterns, security, and even income. It is these losses that contribute to the development of depression.

It is noteworthy that sociological and psychiatric studies have focused on moves in working-class subjects. It is rarely noted in the reports of researchers, most of whom are aspirants in the upward ladder of university and professional career activities, that the geographical moves that are usually part of their own lives may be stressful both to them and their families. The particular components of that stress-

Reprinted and abridged by permission of Transaction Inc. from *Society* 9 (July/August 1972), © 1972 by Transaction Inc. This study was supported by U.S.P.H.S. Grant MH 137838 from N.I.M.H.

fullness may be different in any move. Nevertheless, it would appear that as universal as the experience of moving is in American society, it is also a considerable universal stress and challenge.

During the course of studying a group of depressed women in New Haven, Connecticut, we noted in a number of them temporal relationships between their depressive symptoms and recent moves. These women often did not relate their illnesses to the moves but more often attributed them to other events in their lives, such as financial problems, increased loneliness, increased marital friction, problems with children, career frustrations, identity confusion. In most cases, however, these other events were the by-products of faulty adaptation to the stresses and changes created by moving. We suspected that these women did not associate their symptoms with moving, since it is such an accepted part of American life that it is almost taken for granted. These women instead internalized the stresses and blamed themselves for their problems. The result was an emergence of depressive symptoms.

Most of the women were patients in a research clinic and were being treated for depressive episodes. They showed the usual symptoms of depression, including feelings of helplessness and futility, hopelessness about the future and persistent sadness, impaired capacity to perform their work and other usual activities, and a loss of interest in friends and family. We were led to examine their experience of moving in detail, and we found that in some cases the move was the last straw in a series of stressful events and interpersonal difficulties. In other cases moving represented an abortive effort to solve other problems, often financial or marital. However, in some cases the move itself created new stresses and interpersonal difficulties which had not previously existed. This pattern of depression occurred even though the moves were voluntary and related to presumably desirable circumstances, such as improved housing and financial status. This sharply contrasts with reports suggesting that moves produce detrimental effects only if they are involuntary or undesirable.

The circumstances surrounding the moves and the reasons they occurred showed wide variation and we proceeded to classify them. The following represent some of the different types we encountered and probably cover the most common kinds of moves made each year. Although our examples (drawn primarily from the research clinic which treated only women) are depressed women, we believe that moving also creates stresses for men. Equally, the impact extends beyond the narrow bounds of the depression clinic. We believe we are documenting here a stress which is extremely common, although often ignored or underestimated. Although most studies of the psychological effects of mobility have focused on groups that make up only a small portion of the people who move—such as working-class families who are forced out of their homes by urban renewal or military families who are regularly reassigned to new posts—our study covered a wider socioeconomic range of families. Rather than being confined to lower-class and military families, the impact of moving, we found, was stressful to women of all classes.

The effects of forced dislocation from an urban slum through urban renewal has been well described by Marc Fried in his study of the working-class residents of the West End of Boston. His subjects were people who had a strong and positive attachment to their homes and community, strong interpersonal relations and ties, and a group identity based on availability and contact with familiar groups of people. When the West End homes were torn down for redevelopment and the residents relocated, a majority of the individuals experienced the reaction Fried described as "grieving for a lost home." This grief was manifested in feelings of painful loss, continued longing, helplessness, depressive tone, and a tendency to idealize the lost place. The researcher concluded that while relocation may increase the rate of social mobility and create new opportunities for some people, for most of the working class dislocation leads to intense personal suffering, which is not easily alleviated by larger or newer apartments or by home ownership. Similar experiences have been reported in studies made in England.

In our New Haven study, we found fewer urban renewal victims. But when we did, our findings were consistent with those of the Boston study.

Miss T., a 54-year-old single woman born and raised in Italy, lived with her single brother. She worked as a machine operator and had held this job for the last 14 years. She had lived in central New Haven since she was fifteen and in the same home her father had purchased. After her parents' death she and her brother had stayed on in the house. One year prior to her depressive illness, she and her brother were forced to move out of the house because of the City Redevelopment Program. Together, they purchased a small house in a semi-rural area, without public transportation, about eight miles from the city. She began to feel isolated, extremely lonely and bored in her new home. It was difficult for her to see her friends and relatives, as she did not drive. She missed the familiar neighbors she had known as a youngster, the short walk to the downtown shops and seeing her girlfriends whom she had previously gone out with at least two nights a week. She also had to give up her weekly social club because of lack of transportation. She was not able to warm up to the new parish church which she described as "more beautiful than the old but not so cozy." At first she was enraged towards the city officials for forcing the family to move. Then her anger shifted towards her brother and other family members for their willingness to adapt. Finally, her rage turned inward, when her siblings kept insisting that she should snap out of her depression and adjust as they had. She became fatigued and weepy, lost weight and developed difficulty sleeping. She would come home from work exhausted and go immediately to sleep. She began to feel she would be better off dead.

Decent housing is invariably a major problem for the poor, particularly people on welfare. Welfare recipients are often moved from one place to another against their will. They are often not as concerned about the breakup of their old neighborhoods as about what the new one will be like, realizing that their stay in the neighborhood will probably be short.

Mrs. L., a 29 year-old woman with five young children, was forced to go on welfare when her husband was arrested for drunkenness and beating up the children. He never had been able to support the family in a sustained fashion and when they separated, she assumed all financial support of the children. She lived in a pleasant semi-suburban area when she was not on welfare. Eventually she had to go to an old apartment, in the center of an urban slum, when welfare began to pay the rent. The neighborhood was noisy and there was much crime, fighting and drunkenness. She became extremely apprehensive and nervous for herself and her children. Three weeks prior to her coming for treatment for depression, her 17-month-old son was hospitalized for lead poisoning. She developed insomnia, became hopeless and pessimistic and blamed herself for the difficulties. These feelings continued until she was moved by welfare to a new housing project in a safer neighborhood. . . .

It is easier to change your address than yourself. Some of our patients became depressed when they found that moving did not solve interpersonal problems but created additional ones.

Frequently the problem was related to a conflict-ridden sexual relationship. One woman was carrying on an extramarital affair, which her husband presumably did not know about. When the relationship deepened she was faced with the possibility of having to make a choice between her husband and her lover. She demanded that her husband buy the family a new home in the country, away from the urban duplex housing they had always occupied. The spouse was perplexed by his wife's demands but succumbed to them, although they could hardly afford to move. In the country, the patient's *Better Homes and Gardens* fantasies of homemaking rapidly evaporated. She was lonely, missed the constant visiting back and forth of her friends, and had no money or energy to devote to making the home beautiful. She took to bed, lost 15 pounds, felt depressed, trapped, hopeless, and suicidal.

A lovely private home, grass in which the children can play, clean air, birds, and peace motivate a significant number of Americans each year to voluntarily leave multifamily urban homes and move to the suburbs. Unlike the previous moves we described, which were mostly involuntary and undesirable, the move to the suburbs from the city, from a rented apartment to a private home, symbolizes the family's prosperity and success and is usually considered a joyous event. While opinions differ on the desirability of such a life-style, some researchers have found that suburban life itself had little ill effect on mental health. They did note, however, that certain groups of people find the suburbs stressful. Among them are adolescents, who are consumers of the urban activities and become bored with the lack of activities in the suburbs, working-class women who find it difficult to deal with the social demands of the new environment, urban cosmopolitan individuals who miss the city and feel isolated, and educated women who want to work.

Herbert Gans concludes that people who have problems in the city bring them to the suburbs. We certainly would agree with this conclusion; however, we did find some women who did not fall into any of these groups described as having difficulty in the suburbs. These women could not adapt even though the move was considered desirable by the family. In these cases, it seems that the depressive illness was intensified or exacerbated by the suburban life-style. For example, the low population density and the loss of natural daily social gatherings on the porch, the street, or the corner drug store made sharing experiences and ventilating problems more difficult. Thus more emotional demands were put on the nuclear family, especially on the husband. If the marriage was shaky, the husband unavailable because of long hours at work or emotional disentanglement, the woman felt isolated and alone. Often people of similar age and income lived in the community, especially in the new developments, and no older baby-sitters, or bearers of grandmotherly wisdom were available to the young mother. This was especially difficult for the woman if she had depended on her own mother for support and advice and the move had made daily contacts with her family less possible.

Mrs. Z. was a 37-year-old married woman with two small children. She had married late, in her early 30's, and helped her husband better himself by working herself, so that he could return to college. The couple worked hard together and saved money so that they could someday purchase their own home. After graduation her husband's success as an accountant continued and he received enough of a salary increase so that their dream could be realized. The family moved to a new ranch home in the suburbs about 15 miles from the urban area where they had lived. With the cost of moving and setting up their new home they could not afford a second car so that Mrs. Z. was unable to leave the home during the day and visit her mother or sisters whom she had been used to seeing daily. She had always been a shy and insecure woman and found it difficult to establish friendships with her neighbors. In the past when she had felt blue or lonesome she would go to her local pharmacist, an older kindly man, sit on a stool in his drug store and talk to him. Now, alone in the house, without her family in daily contact and with her neighbors occupied with their own young families, she felt alone and unable to cope with the new house or her children. When she complained to her parents they scolded her for being ungrateful and not appreciating her new home. Her husband saw the house as a symbol of his "arriving" and became obsessed with it, seeking out more chores in his spare time in order to maintain and improve the house. Mrs. Z. felt she was slipping into second place as he became annoyed with her complaints.

In some cases, the move to the suburbs put unanticipated financial burdens on the family which considerably increased the tension in the home. In purchasing the home, the extra cost of commuting, the second car, baby-sitters who previously had been neighbors or family in the building, the care of the grass, and recreation for the children had not been considered. While some families thrived on the shared chores in the new home, for some families it was a burden which frequently fell to the woman, leading to her feelings of resentment and futility.

The R.'s had been married five years when they decided to move to the suburbs. Their marriage had gone fairly well those first five years. However, financial problems began to mount as a result of this move, as unanticipated problems with the house occurred—the water supply was inadequate and they had to dig another well. Even after that the water was poor. They incurred many bills and couldn't afford furniture for the house or recreation. Mrs. R. found living out in the country isolating. She missed her neighbors and friends and as a result had more expectations and desire of companionship from her husband than he was able to supply. Her nagging was beginning to drive him away and she feared that he was unfaithful.

Career advancement in many professions and in academia often depends on the individual's willingness to move to a better job. In fact, the middle-class professional has become a new migrant worker, especially during the early years of his career. One recent study of 280 university faculty wives indicated that the typical family moved on the average of three times in ten years and that two-thirds of these moves meant an upward step for the husband's career. For his wife it can have considerably different implications. One research group has reported on the discrepancy between spouses in the perception of moving. They considered why a group of similar persons, in this instance the husbands of depressed women who were subjected to the same stress of moving did not develop the same symptoms of depression. They noted that the event of moving, necessitated by a job change, was usually initiated by the husband who viewed it quite differently from his wife. The husband felt he was initiator, but the wife felt helpless and a victim. This discrepancy in perception may be less frequent in families who have fallen on hard times and who see the move as an active solution to an already poor situation. But in the middle-class family the wife may not see enough tangible financial or social improvement to offset the disruption of moving. Further, if the man is preoccupied with his career he may not assist in the move, and the burden of selling the house, finding a new one, and making friends falls to his wife.

The B's were a prosperous couple in their late 30s with two children of school age. Mr. B. was an insurance executive who had risen steadily in the company from selling insurance to a responsible administrative job. His advancement had necessitated four moves in the past five years, in most cases to a new state. The pattern of the moves was always the same. Mr. B would go ahead of the family. Mrs. B. would stay behind, check the children out of school, sell the house, and move. She resented being left behind with all the work to do. With her last move she felt physically exhausted and found it difficult to make friends. The demanding responsibilities of her husband's new job required that he be away from home often. Mrs. B. missed the friends she had made in the part-time job she had before the move. She was unable easily to find another job in the new community and was too busy unpacking and settling the children in the new school to explore many possibilities. She began to feel hopeless and despondent. . . .

It would seem that the stressful effects of American geographical mobility have been underestimated. Moving often places inordinate demands on the individual to adapt and raises continued challenges to his identity. While many people move each year and experience no problems or only transient ones, there are a substantial number of persons who do experience incapacitating suffering.

An Uprooted Woman: Mrs. Phillips

Mrs. Phillips is in her late forties, a bit heavy, pleasant and outgoing in manner. She has two daughters, one at home, the other, at the time of her account, a secretary to an airline executive. Her story begins with the acceptance by her husband of the attractive job offer that brought them to the city in which the older daughter worked.

My husband was a typical business executive, very dedicated. And he was away most of the time. As far as family life was concerned, we had very little, because he was always traveling. When it was mumps or measles time he was never home. And when he *was* home, he would eat his dinner and about nine o'clock he'd get his briefcase and work until about two in the morning and get up the next morning at six to go to work.

So when this opportunity came up and he knew the people and he liked this type of thing, and he wouldn't have the pressures that he had before, we thought why not go ahead with it. Actually I had mixed emotions and it took him about six months to convince me that this was what we should do. But he did it in a nice way. It wasn't one of these pressure things. And the more I thought about it, the more I realized that we should come here. But I didn't come here very enthusiastically.

In Mrs. Phillips' previous community she had been extremely active socially, and while she had missed her husband because his job kept him on the road so much, her social life had been gratifying.

I was a joiner. I was a Sunday school primary teacher. I had a Girl Scout Brownie troop. I was a Grey Lady. Any time there was a solicitation, a cancer drive or whatever, I was in charge of that for my neighborhood.

We did quite a bit of entertaining. We would have a yearly party with my husband's office. And when my older daughter was home—she was a sorority girl—our house was large enough and our yard was large enough so we could have big parties. I would have eighty teenagers, and it's amazing, I mean it sounds like, "My goodness!" but the young people were very well mannered and we would have a Coke machine downstairs. I would make popcorn and then we'd have outdoor barbecue like hot dogs, and they'd have the record players and play the music that they wanted to play. I would have two or three other mothers and their husbands over at the same time so that we wouldn't have complete charge, but it was very delightful and I loved everything.

People always seemed to feel very warm in my house. Like my duplicate bridge club, when there was a party it was always understood that it would be at my house. One would bring a salad and one would bring this other kind of thing and so on.

There was a round of parties before they left:

We were entertained very extensively and, in fact, we were on the go so much that by the time I got here I was delighted for a few days just to relax.

They had already decided to try to find a house not too far from the airport so that the older daughter could live at home. One middle-income suburb seemed to be perfectly located. It was halfway between Mr. Phillip's new firm and the airport, with good highways running to each. They rented a

AN UPROOTED WOMAN: MRS. PHILLIPS

large house and then, almost immediately, their daughter developed plans of her own.

One of the things we thought was that when we moved here my older daughter, who is twenty-one, would live with us. The reason we moved into this suburb was that it was in easy reach of the airport and my older daughter worked there, so this would make it easy for her to live with us. Well, as soon as we signed the papers on the house she decided that the love bug had bitten her and she had to get married right away. He is a very nice boy, but still, we miss her.

The suburb, chosen for its location, proved uncongenial. The residents were different from the Phillips: they were younger, and their children were younger; they were much more familistic and much less involved in social activities. As just one indication of the Phillips' being out of place, the dominant religion in the suburb was different from their own, so that they had to attend church in another community. The networks available to Mrs. Phillips did not attract her: "They have nothing in common with me."

They were kind to me when we moved in. They brought me cupcakes and one brought me some flowers, potted, you know. Plants. But the people are much younger. There is a real nice girl living next door, but she has seven little children. She doesn't have time to visit. And there is absolutely no activity whatsoever here, absolutely nothing. And we moved in in the winter, when you don't meet anyone. The nearest church that we can attend is in the next town. Not that we are overly religious, don't misunderstand me, but we feel that this is very much a part of our lives.

There is nothing here. These people live in their own small worlds. Their idea of a conversation is, "What are we going to have for dinner?" This is a nice neighborhood, don't misunderstand me. The people are very nice. The man down the street is the manager of the bank here, for example. But they are younger—I am forty-eight—and naturally they have nothing in common with me. They have small children, and some have four or five of them.

Mrs. Phillips began to suffer the painful, nagging, boredom of social isolation. She became painfully aware of the contrast between her current situation and her previous life. Grief for her loss accentuated her loneliness.

This is something I have never been confronted with before. We had a group that we'd known for years. We had all had our children at the same time. We had so much in common. I had so many friends that would occasionally drop in, and I always knew that I could call someone. It is a pretty horrible feeling to be in a place and be alone, not knowing anyone and not having anyone to talk to. Where we used to live, if I got real bored I could call somebody and talk to them over the phone. I didn't necessarily have to see them. But to be in a place where you don't know anyone at all, you just have this loneliness, you just feel like it is just coming in on top of you and you can't do anything about it.

Mrs. Phillips attempted symbolically to hang on to her former community by writing. In a way, she was seeking to regain her lost network. Writing had some value—though it hardly met her needs.

For a while, I would write three or four letters a day, some to friends that I enjoyed, but that I did not feel very close to, but just knowing that they would answer a letter so that I would hear from them.

It wasn't quite the case that there was no one with whom Mrs. Phillips could become friendly. There was another woman, about her age, who lived not far from her, and who wanted very much to be her friend. But one friend is not a community, and, as it happened, this friend was an alcoholic. Mrs. Phillips was genuinely concerned about her own attraction to alcohol.

I have this neighbor down the street who works, but Wednesday she has off, and always on Wednesday she calls and says come on over, this is my day off. Well, she is an alcoholic, and that doesn't help the situation at all, because I can feel myself becoming one right along with her, just due to the fact of not having anything to do.

I find myself on the verge of alcoholism. Being completely bored, I go to the refrigerator—we always have beer and wine —and I have a glass of wine.

I could become an alcoholic. I find myself, to be completely honest, fighting it. I enjoy a drink, but normally, I am far from being an alcoholic. But now I find myself in the daytime or at noon, I go to the pantry and find myself something. Now this is not good. It is just during the day. I find as soon as my daughter gets home from school, I am okay. Just as long as someone is in the house.

I can sympathize with the people who have gone through this kind of thing because I can see exactly what will happen unless I can conquer it. There is nothing like being honest. I have this cohort who is helping me along with it, which doesn't help the situation either. I think, "Well, maybe today I won't have anything," and she comes over and I have a beer or something like that and before I know it, I am sitting out having two or three beers.

And then I think, "Oh well, I won't tomorrow." And then tomorrow comes and I start drinking again, and before I know it, it's tomorrow and tomorrow and tomorrow. Life is too short for this kind of thing.

Connected to the incipient alcoholism were sleep problems. Mrs. Phillips was too tense to sleep at night. During the day she cherished sleep as an escape.

At night I don't sleep. I am just so emotionally upset that at night my mind is going a million miles an hour and I resent the fact of Neil lying over there snoring when I can't sleep. So I think if maybe I take another glass I'll get real sleep. And then I'll think, "Now this is absolutely absurd!" But sometimes around noontime I might think that if I took maybe another glass, I'd get real sleepy. Or if a fit of depression was coming on, I would say to myself, "I'll take this and I'll sleep." To tell the truth, I sleep a lot. In fact, I have never slept so much before in my life.

And there were other problems as well, perhaps less serious.

The biggest problem has been alcoholism. But I have had indigestion problems. And I thought I was having a heart attack even though I knew darned good and well I wasn't. Another thing, I've been talking to the dog. As long as he doesn't answer, I guess I'm all right.

It was perplexing to Mrs. Phillips that the relationship with her husband did not help. She felt, at times, that the absence of community was her own fault—but then quickly shifted to feeling that her isolation was unjust and pitiable.

I can't say I'm not loved, because I am. It is just these crazy emotional things. You start feeling you're not wanted, you start feeling sorry for yourself. I'll be quite honest. I've been feeling quite sorry for myself.

Mr. Phillips sympathized with his wife and did what he could to brighten her mood. But no matter what he did, it wasn't enough. A husband's companionship is far better than no companionship at all, but it does not satisfy the need for a community.

He is so kind. I mean, he takes me out to dinner and he tries to do things that make me happy. But he can't do anything right as far as I am concerned. I am belligerent to him and he gets so hurt, and I think this is what happens in a situation like this. I am not living a normal life. I take all my gripes out on the only person around.

When we came here, knowing how badly he wanted to come, I was afraid to say to Neil what I actually felt because I didn't want him to know how unhappy I was. I held back a little on things that ordinarily I would have said.

Women need a woman to talk to, they really do. It's because women understand women. You feel that you just have to have somebody to let your hair down with and say just what you actually feel. But I have no one now.

Instead of bringing Mrs. Phillips closer to her spouse, the absence of community caused her to express irritation. She was angry at her husband for his inability to help and was envious of his contacts with others.

You've read enough, you're tired of reading, you're tired of knitting and TV, so you sit. And all of a sudden you're talking to yourself mentally. And you can build it up until, before you know it, it's boiling, ready to erupt. About the time it is ready to erupt is the time that your husband comes home. So you start in, "Now don't put your pipe there, I just cleaned that today." "Now watch that, Neil, be sure and hang up your coat." "Now, did you go to the laundry today?" "What did you have for lunch?" "Who did you see?" And a million questions before the man even has a chance to sit down.

Fortunately Neil has a disposition that rather than explode, he goes right along and is very calm. He's a very calm individual. He goes right along with it. And here I want to hear every detail of his day, and I hate every minute of it, I want to hear it, but when he tells me, I get mad all the time for the fact that why didn't I go? Why couldn't I see so and so? Why didn't I go into town? I wanted to hear it, but when I did hear it, I'd just be sorry for myself.

Mrs. Phillips began to feel distant from her husband. Just as social isolation becomes a secondary development of emotional isolation among the widowed and separated, emotional isolation may follow social isolation among the uprooted. Mrs. Phillips thought that if she and her husband had been younger, they could have reached each other in bed. Perhaps so, but, as Weissman and Paykel report, younger couples encounter similar sorts of estrangement under the pressures of social isolation.

At our age we're over the sexual life that young people have. When you are young, sex is most important, but when you get older those things wane. Sure, a love pat and a kiss mean a great deal, but it's not the same as when you are a twenty-one-year old girl. So you don't have this to rely on. When you are young you can get into a big fight and everything can go wrong, and then your husband can make love to you and all is forgiven. Well, as you grow older, you don't have this type of relationship. It's a deeper thing. So you get this thing welling up in you and you have no way of getting it out other than just a complete explosion, which I don't want to give in to.

In a somewhat different way, Mrs. Phillips' relationship with her younger daughter was being spoiled. Mrs. Phillips couldn't tell her daughter about her distress and couldn't help her daughter deal with her own social isolation.

I see Bonnie dying a slow death. The poor girl just comes home and she doesn't say anything, but she looks at me as if to say, "Why did you do this to me?"

I don't want Bonnie to know my feelings because I can see how unhappy she is and I don't want to burden her with more. So I keep it in rather than letting it out with her.

Finally Mrs. Phillips decided they had to move. A bit of medical advice probably played a role in her decision.

Bonnie was lying around the house and I felt that something was wrong because she was acting not as a teen-ager should act. Immediately I thought she had some kind of anemia. So I went and took her to the doctor and he gave her a thorough physical and said that he wished all young girls that age could be as healthy. Then he took me in and said that it was due to this move and that she was bored. So I was thinking about moving and I asked him what he thought another move would do, and he said, "Well, if you move now it would be fine, but if you wait a year, you'll have to go through this again."

With that opinion as incentive, Mrs. Phillips began an intensive campaign to find a community where she would be comfortable. It took her only about two weeks to locate a community that not only was attractive but also had the right churches, a modern hospital, and an office of the Red Cross in the main street. She and her husband broke their lease on the house they had been renting, paid a month's rent as a penalty, and a month later moved for the second time. This time the move was successful.

Before we moved, I occupied my time with just cleaning house. But now I have lovely neighbors. My neighbor next door has a flower garden and a vegetable garden so I have not had to buy a fresh vegetable since I have been here. We have been to church every Sunday. I'm near the shopping center. I have joined the Women's Club, and I'll be working as a volunteer at the Hospital. I've also joined the League of Women Voters.

When we came here I went out to the hospital and talked to the volunteers. They have ward aides, like the Grey Ladies, but you don't wear the uniform of a Grey Lady. And then the girl across the street said to me one day, "I belong to the League of Women Voters. Would you like to join?" And I said I'd love to.

Where we were before, there was nothing to join, nothing to do. Here, for instance, there was a coffee across the street at eleven this morning. And my neighbor next door two weeks ago had a party and had eight couples in so that we could meet all the new neighbors. They are just as charming and just as warm—they are people that you walk in and feel like you are known. It's not like meeting a cold blank wall.

If I go into a store, I've been here long enough now so when I go in, I'm recognized. And I have this wonderful shopping center. So I have no time to be bored.

In her new setting, with social isolation at an end, Mrs. Phillips' fears of alcoholism vanished, as did her difficulties with sleeping. Her relationships with her husband and daughter improved markedly. Her husband was relieved to see her once again her old self. Her daughter, like her, found the new setting congenial and was quickly caught up in a teen-age social circle.

When we saw Mrs. Phillips in her first residence she appeared drawn and extraordinarily tense. She spoke quickly, her words pushing one another, as though they were under pressure. When we saw her later, in her second residence, she still spoke quickly, but now with more control. Her mood had brightened dramatically. She displayed a bubbling self-confidence and optimism where earlier there had been self-doubt and barely concealed anxiety. One would hardly have expected a change in neighborhood to make such a difference. But then, it wasn't really the neighborhood that was the issue, but rather integration as opposed to isolation.

Isolation and Loneliness in the Aged

Peter Townsend

To be socially isolated is to have few contacts with family and community; to be lonely is to have an unwelcome *feeling* of lack or loss of companionship. The one is objective, the other subjective, and, as we shall see, the two do not coincide.

Social isolation needs to be measured by reference to objective criteria. The problem is rather like that of measuring poverty. "Poverty" is essentially a relative rather than an absolute term, and discovering its extent in a population is usually divided into two stages. Most people agree on the first stage, which is to place individuals on a scale according to their income; they often disagree about the second, which involves deciding how far up the scale the poverty "line" should be drawn. The task of measuring isolation can also be divided in this way by placing individuals on a scale according to their degree of isolation and by drawing a line at some point on the scale so that those below the line would, by common consent, be called "the isolated."

It is no easy task. One man works in a factory, lives with his wife and children, goes to the cinema and the pub regularly each week, and is secretary to a poultry club which meets

From Peter Townsend, *The Family Life of Old People,* abridged edition (London: Penguin Books, 1963), pp. 188–205.

each weekend. Another man lives alone because his wife is dead, has retired from work, visits a married daughter every day, spends his weekends with a son, and meets his friends in the park. How can these two men be placed on a common scale? The method suggested here is crude and tentative, but perhaps it can be developed into something more systematic.

It is based on information about old people's social contacts, particularly their contacts with relatives. By *contact* is meant a meeting with another person, usually prearranged or customary at home or outside, which involves more than a casual exchange of greetings between, say, two neighbors in the street. The first step was to add together the average number of contacts a week with each relative, some of whom, of course, were seen together; the second was to add on contacts with nonrelatives, mainly neighbors and friends but also, for example, district nurses, home helps, and doctors; the third was to add on an arbitrarily chosen score for other social activities in the week. Thus a weekly visit to a club, to the cinema, or to church was given a score of 2; a full-time occupation was given a weekly score of 20, a part-time occupation 10. An example is given at the top of the next page.

The difficulties of applying this method must not be underrated. For one thing, no account was taken of the function, intensity, or duration of the contact: the score for a visit to another person, for example, was the same whether it lasted five minutes or three hours. A relative or nonrelative living at home was given twice the score of a person seen daily, that is 14. Irregular contacts, such as annual holidays with distant relatives, were averaged out on a weekly basis

Widow Living Alone	Number of Social Contacts per Week
One married and one widowed daughter seen daily	14
Two grandchildren seen daily	14
Son-in-law seen once a week	1
Sister seen once a week	1
Two married sons, their wives and three children seen once a week	7
Brother and wife seen every fortnight ($\frac{1}{2} + \frac{1}{2}$)	1
Twelve other relatives seen from once to six times a year	1
Part-time occupation as school cleaning woman	10
Visit to old people's club once a week	2
Neighbor exchanging visits twice a week	2
Irregular social activities (doctor, monthly, visit to cinema, etc.)	1
Total score	**54**

for the year as a whole. Such contacts were generally of small importance, compared with the number occurring regularly, every day or every week. This is largely why, on balance, this method of scoring social contacts seemed to be feasible at least in this district. Day-by-day contacts with relatives formed the major part of the social world of these old people. Many of them, in any case, had a limited range of social activities because of infirmity. [See Table 1 on the next page.]

Table 1. Social Isolation of Old People

Degree of isolation	Old people Per cent-age	Number	Social contacts per week Mean	Median
Not isolated	77	156	72–79	67
Rather isolated[a]	13	27	29–31	28
Isolated[b]	10	20	14–16	17
Total	100	203	61–63	52

[a] 25–35 contacts per week (or between 3 and 5 per day).
[b] 21 or fewer contacts per week (or 3 or less per day).

The weekly social contact score for each individual represented the extent of an individual's isolation from, or involvement in, family and society. The scores of the 203 people in the sample were listed on a continuous scale, the highest, 208, being at the top and the lowest, 2, at the bottom. Examples will show the variations in social activities underlying these scores.

A married woman of sixty-four lived with her husband, a single son, and a granddaughter. She had a part-time occupation as an office cleaner. Three married daughters lived nearby and she saw them and four of their children every day. She saw two of their husbands nearly every day and one once a week, her eldest son and his wife only once or twice a week. The surviving members of the husband's family were not seen, but two of the wife's nieces called every fortnight. She had a widowed friend living alone whom she visited once a fortnight but she took pride in not having any regular association with a neighbor. She went to the cinema once or twice a month. *Total score 124.*

A married man of sixty-nine lived with his wife. He had a full-time job as a nightwatchman. He attended a club once a week, went to the cinema once a fortnight, and met two friends in a local pub two or three times a week. His only child, a daughter, lived nearby with her husband and child, and he saw the three of them every day. Most of his surviving brothers and sisters lived abroad, but he saw two of them and their children a few times each year. He saw three of his wife's brothers and their families from once a month to once a fortnight at weekends. *Total score 69.*

A widow aged seventy-eight lived alone in a tenement flat. She had no children, had lost touch with her husband's family after his death fifteen years previously, and had not seen her surviving brother for some years. Two of a dead sister's three children lived nearby. Seeing them was her chief social activity. One married niece had two children and her household included her unmarried brother. The widow visited them two afternoons a week and the unmarried nephew also called on her once or twice a week. Another niece lived in another section of London and the widow visited her every other weekend for an afternoon. Otherwise she had no regular association with friends, neighbors, or relatives. She did not go to church or to a club, but went to a cinema two or three times a week, alone. *Total score 18.*

The people at the bottom of the scale merit close attention. They were usually living alone, older than average, without children or other relatives living nearby, retired from work, and infirm. It was the combination of three or more of these factors that produced social isolation rather than any single one. Many of the oldest and most infirm people in the sample had a secure and rich family life. Many living alone saw a great deal of relatives and friends nearby. Some with no children were at work and had close relationships with brothers and sisters and nephews and nieces.

The ten most isolated people of the 203 interviewed were all unmarried or childless. **The circumstances of one is summarized below.**

Mr. Fortune, aged seventy-six, lived alone in a two-room council flat. There were two wooden chairs, an orange-box converted into a cupboard, a gas stove, a table covered with newspaper, a battered old pram with tins and boxes inside, a pair of wooden steps, and little else in the sitting-room. There was no fire, although the interview took place on a cold February morning. Mr. Fortune had been a cripple from birth and he was partly deaf. He was unmarried and his five siblings were dead. An older widowed sister-in-law lived about a mile away with an unmarried son and daughter. These three and two married nieces living in another borough were seen from once a month to a few times a year. Asked how often he saw his sister-in-law Mr. Fortune said, "Only when I go there. It's a hard job to walk down there in winter time and I haven't seen her for three or four months." Asked about an old people's club he said, "No, I'm simply as I am now. I shouldn't like to join. Walking is such a painful job for me. I can't get any amusement out of it." He spoke to one or two of the neighbors outside his flat but he had no regular contact with any of them. He had one regular friend, living a few blocks away, who came over to see him on a Sunday about once a month, "More when there's fine weather." He was not a churchgoer, never went to a cinema, rarely went to a pub because he could not afford a drink, had never had a holiday in his life, and spent Christmas on his own. "My nephew came down for an hour. He gave me a little present. No, I didn't get any cards." He received a pension and supplementary assistance through the National Assistance Board, which recently arranged for him to have a woman help in his home for two hours a week. Her regular call was the main event of the week. "I sit here messing about. Last week I was making an indoor aerial. I made those steps over there. I like listening to the wireless and making all manner of things. My time's taken up, I can tell you, with that and cooking and tidying up."

The most striking fact about the most isolated people was that they had few surviving relatives, particularly close relatives of their own or of succeeding generations.... The isolated included a comparatively high number of unmarried and childless people, of those possessing sons but not daughters, and of those without siblings. Rarely did they have friends, become members of clubs, or otherwise participate in outside social activities in compensation. Nearly all of them were retired, and most were infirm; some were shy of revealing to others how ill or poverty-stricken they were or how they had "let themselves go." They had little or no means of regular contact with the younger generation, and for one reason or another could not be brought into club activities.

LONELINESS IN OLD AGE

So far the circumstances of isolated people have been described without indicating how far they experienced feelings of loneliness. One of the most striking results of the whole inquiry was that those living in relative isolation from family and community did not always say they were lonely.

Particular importance was attached during the interviews to "loneliness." The question was not asked until most of an individual's activities had been discussed, and care was taken to ensure as serious and as considered a response as possible. One difficulty had to be overcome. A few people liked to let their children think they were lonely so the latter would visit them as much as possible. This meant they were not inclined to give an honest answer if children were present. In an early interview one married woman, asked whether she ever got lonely, said, "Sometimes I do when they are all at work." But she hesitated before answering and looked at two married daughters, who were in the room. On a subsequent call, when this woman was alone, she told me she was "never lonely really, but I like my children to call." A widow, who was alone when interviewed, said she was never lonely. In fascinating contrast to this was a statement of one of her married daughters, who was interviewed independently. "She's not too badly off. The most she complains of is loneliness. She's always wanting us to go up there." Care was therefore taken to ask about loneliness so far as possible when the old person was alone and to check any answer which seemed doubtful.

Some people living at the center of a large family complained of loneliness, and some who were living in extreme isolation repeated several times with vigor that they were never lonely—like Mr. Fortune, described above. The relation between isolation and loneliness is shown in Table 2. Despite there being a significant association, about a half of the isolated and rather isolated said they were not lonely; over a fifth of the first group said they were.

What is the explanation? Previous investigations have pointed to the multiplicity of causes of loneliness. In his Wolverhampton study Sheldon showed that those experiencing loneliness tended to be widowed and single people, to be living alone, to be in their eighties rather than in their sixties, to be men rather than women, and to be the relatively infirm. There seemed to be no single cause of severe loneliness in old

Table 2. Social Isolation and Loneliness (in percentages)

Old People Saying They Were	Not Isolated	Rather Isolated	Isolated [a]	All Old People (Number)
Very lonely	3	15	10	5
Sometimes lonely	18	41	30	22
Not lonely	79	44	60	72
Total	100	100	100	100
Number	156	27	20	203

[a] As defined in Table 1

people. He concluded, "Loneliness cannot be regarded as the simple direct result of social circumstances, but is rather an individual response to an external situation to which other people may react quite differently." He added, in parenthesis, that the main exception to this statement was when the death of a spouse was recent.[1]

In several respects the present inquiry reached similar results. Forty-six percent of widowed people said they were very or sometimes lonely, forty-two percent of those living alone, fifty-three percent of those in their late seventies and eighties, and forty-three percent of those who were infirm, compared with twenty-seven percent in the sample as a whole. But it is possible that less emphasis should be given to personal differences and to a multiplicity of causes. The results also suggested that a single social factor may be fundamental to loneliness. This is the recent deprivation of the company of a close relative, usually a husband or wife or a child, through death, illness, or migration.

RECENT BEREAVEMENT

Examination of individual interview reports showed that of the 56 people saying they were very or sometimes lonely, 28 had been recently bereaved and 17 separated from children. This seemed to be the chief cause of their loneliness. A further 11 had experienced other drastic changes in family circumstances. It is necessary to consider these lonely people.

All but 4 of the 28 who had been recently bereaved had lost a husband or wife within the previous ten years. "No one knows what loneliness is till your partner happens to go." "You don't realize it until you know it. But loneliness is the worst thing you can suffer in life." The men in particular talked about their bereavement with very deep feeling. "I miss her. Every time I look over there—that's her seat. People kept telling me to have someone to look after me but I said to myself, there'll never be another woman who will take her place." Three of them did not talk, they wept.

Mr. Heart had lost his wife seven years earlier. He lived with an unmarried son but he had no daughter. "Sometimes I get lonely. I think of her. There's not a day passes but she's in my mind. When she died I don't know how I stood on my feet. You don't know what it is when you don't have a wife. . . . I wish I had a daughter. If you had a daughter it would put you in mind of your wife. . . . You can't tell how you miss someone until they go. Death's a terrible thing, to lose someone you love."

One of the major consequences of a wife's death was that the man saw less of his children. He acknowledged it was the mother who held the family together. "My daughters used to come round often when my wife was alive, but I don't see so much of them now. But they like to know I'm comfortable and being looked after." Widowers in fact saw less of their children, particularly of their sons, than married men and married or widowed women, as judged by average frequency of contact. But this falling-off did not apply to all a widower's children. A close relationship with one child was usually maintained. Several lived with a single married daughter, or visited a married daughter daily, and then described the pleasure grandchildren gave them. "My young granddaughter likes swinging and I pick her up and she swings between my legs. And then she climbs up on me. Playing with my grandchildren is my greatest pleasure." They found some consolation here. "I'm a grandfather," said one man, "and that's the only goodness I get out of life."

The loss of the marriage partner was not such a disaster for women. They had always depended less on husbands than husbands on them, and they found it easier to console themselves with their families. Nevertheless, many of them were lonely, particularly if their husbands had died recently and particularly if infirmity or shortage of relatives prevented them from finding comfort readily in the companionship of others. One woman's husband had died eight years previously. She had no children. "I get so lonely I could fill up the teapot with tears."

Mrs. Pridy was very infirm and her husband had died only a year previously, when she was eighty. She lived with a daughter and grandchildren. "I sit here for hours and hours sometimes thinking about it. I get depressed and I start crying. We was always together. I can remember even his laughing. "Come on, girl," he'd say, "don't get sitting about. Let's liven 'em up." They say what is to be will be. I never thought he'd . . . . I sit here for hours thinking about him. I can't get over it."

Almost every man and woman whose husband or wife had died within the previous five years, compared with a half between five and ten years and a quarter over that limit, felt lonely. The shorter the period since the death, the more likely were people to complain of loneliness. Although practically everyone felt lonely at first, after about five or six years the presence or not of an affectionate family seemed to determine how long such feeling persisted.

Four people had lost a child and not a husband recently. Three were women widowed in the 1914 war who said a son had died in the previous few years. One had lost two sons in the 1939 war and another three years previously. "I could cry my heart out sometimes when I sit here." There was also a married woman whose only son had been killed at Arnhem in 1944. "He's never out of my mind. I always see him in my mind and they're still talking about wars." In speaking of the loss of children and other relatives it was notable how long people felt grief and how indelible was the memory of these people.

RECENT SEPARATION

After bereavement, recent separation from children and grandchildren was the most important reason for loneliness. . . .

Mrs. Foreman had been a widow for over thirty years. She had no daughters and until twelve months previously had been living with her married son. He had now moved to a new housing estate. Although she stayed with him every weekend she was lonely at home. "I don't like coming back here...."

There remained a number whose loneliness seemed to be due to other causes. All had recently experienced a marked change in their social circumstances. The husband of one and the daughter of another were in hospital and had been there for some months. A third complained bitterly about the new council flat to which she had been moved a year previously; she was among neighbors she did not know or like and she was farther from two of her relatives. Two married men were infirm and could not leave the house; both had retired within the past three years. A married woman had experienced several drastic changes in the past few years and was one of the most lonely of all those interviewed. As an extreme example, she is worth noting.

Mrs. Austin, in her late sixties, lived in a council flat with her husband. She said she missed not having her seven children around her and that she was "very lonely. I can't account for it at all. I get so depressed." Five of the seven had married within a space of three years around 1950 and had left home one after another. All but two had moved [quite far away; though within the metropolitan area]. These two lived about a mile way. One son, to whom she was particularly attached, had been killed in an accident several years previously. Soon after the children had married Mr. and Mrs. Austin had to leave their home, because it was to be demolished. "I can't settle here. I'd been over forty years in one house. Since it's been pulled down and we've come here I've hardly spoken to my next-door neighbors. All the old neighbors have gone. You can't go in and out like you used to." She saw much less of her children than formerly, although her two youngest visited her twice a week and three of the others once a fortnight. Her only sister had died three years ago. Because of headaches she could no longer knit. Her husband had been in ill health for several years and was on bad terms with some of the children. Mrs. Austin had made two attempts at suicide and had recently spent six months in a mental hospital.

In this example nearly all the disturbing social changes that can occur in the life of an old person had occurred. Close relatives had died, the children had migrated, the old home and neighborhood had to be given up, and many activities had to be abandoned because of increasing infirmity. This was desolation with a vengeance.

NOTE

1. J. H. Sheldon, *The Social Medicine of Old Age,* Report of an inquiry in Wolverhampton. (London: Oxford University Press, 1948).

6

Responses
to Loneliness

Introduction

How might the lonely deal with their condition? Many strategies would seem possible.

They might try to get those still available to them to supply the currently missing provisions; a newcomer couple, for example, might turn to one another for the companionship each would normally expect from friendships; or a man recently separated from his wife might bring his ups and downs to a married sister. But ordinarily it would seem that these attempts to find new provisions in old ties prove disappointing. Relationships are not so easily modified; they are constrained by previous underlying assumptions, by the inherent interactional limitations of the participants, and by the participants' competing commitments. The newcomer wife may discover there is little gratification in discussing pediatricians with her husband; he has too little store of experience, and too different a set of current concerns. The separated man may discover that he cannot bring his troubles to his sister as he had to his wife; his sister has her own husband and children to care for before she has time for him.

Among the lonely many grit their teeth and attempt to see it through all by themselves. There may appear to them and to others to be more dignity in this and less risk of new rejection and humiliation. Yet this is an acceptance of isolation: an acceptance, at least for a time, of the impossibility of bridging the gulf between themselves and others. Some go as far as they can with this; they withdraw from others physically as well as emotionally, sequester themselves, and as far as is possible live alone with their loneliness.

Most attempt to establish new relationships. There would seem to be two different ways of going about this. The first is to create an adequate relational life by integrating new relationships into one's existent relational fabric. For example, a man previously without attachment may marry someone who then will become friendly with his friends, a daughter-in-law to his mother, and so on. Insofar as these relationships achieve patterns common in his social world and can be integrated with existing relationships, it is useful to refer to the new relationships as natural ones. An alternative, however, might be for individuals to enter what might be termed *supplementary relationships,* that is, relationships that are not elements of the normal relational patterns of those in their situation, but which are instead consciously designed to make provisions that they could not otherwise obtain. The man without attachment might enter psychotherapy; the woman without a friendship network might enter a newcomers' club.

Supplementary relationships tend to be understood as of limited duration, though this is not necessarily the case. Sometimes they are formed with professionals whose services are in demand and therefore can be furnished only for limited periods. Sometimes they are provided by such groups as newcomers' clubs, whose transitional nature is part of their definition. But something like volunteer work might function as a supplementary relationship for a newcomer and yet could, if desired, be continued indefinitely.

Not only may individuals enter single supplementary relationships to provide relational elements missing from their lives but also they may enter supplementary communities in which a variety of supplementary relationships may be formed. Such communities may be especially useful to those who have experienced multiple failures of relationships as a result of a disastrous event—a marital separation, for example—and want for a time to be able to escape the frustrations of their ongoing lives. Parents Without Partners constitutes such a supplementary community for many individuals, and in the second paper to follow we consider its many provisions to its membership. Before presenting that material, however, we first consider the way in which an individual might rely on a natural ongoing community of friends and kin to manage despair and then to help in the repair of a disrupted life pattern. The benefits of supplementary communities and relationships can then be assessed in comparison with this more usual approach to relational deficit.

The individual who serves as a case example of reliance on one's natural community is a woman called Mrs. Davis. A man who had been her boyfriend for a year and a half, whom she had thought she would marry, had left her. She turned to those close to her, especially her kin, to help her first with her grief and later with her anger. Then after these feelings had abated and she began to deal with loneliness a sister arranged to re-establish a link between her and her former boyfriend. And not long after this the same sister arranged a meeting between her and a new man with whom she rather soon formed a new attachment.

Worth noting in this discussion is the responsiveness to her emotional state of the people with whom Mrs. Davis maintained other relationships: her sisters and her brother, her mother, her friends, her employers. They provided understanding, sympathy, and reassurance, and while relationships with them could not substitute for the relationship that had been lost, they did provide both support and eventually an introduction to a new man with whom a new attachment did form.

It was of great importance that the man to whom Mrs. Davis was introduced was already a member of her ongoing community, linked to her brother-in-law occupationally, to her sister by friendship. These linkages provided both Mrs. Davis and the man with some sense of the other's history and background and with assurance of the other's trustworthiness. They could explore the possibility of attachment without worry lest they be fooled. In general, relationships that are embedded in one's community begin with some mutual assurance of the other's trustworthiness. The community in its collective memory maintains a dossier on its members and appropriate inquiry will usually make the contents of the dossier available.

Supplementary relationships, such as those formed within Parents Without Partners, are ordinarily without linkages to the remainder of an individual's relational fabric. They may be formed with less consequence—no one else need know, at least at first—but they also are formed with less knowledge of the other and ordinarily less trust. They are very likely poorer long-term risks, and because of this they are apt to be entered cautiously, thus increasing their likelihood of failure.

There are advantages to supplementary relationships as well as disadvantages. One is that their isolation from one's ongoing relational fabric makes it possible to begin anew within them, to try out a new self without battling the expectations of those who have known one for years and years. In addition that new self, if it should work out badly, will not be a source of continuing embarrassment in one's ongoing world. Indeed nothing one does or says in a therapist's office, or in an encounter group, is apt to result in immediate social damage, although insofar as these are relationships in which one's emotions are engaged, there is potential for impact on one's spirit and one's self.

Because supplementary relationships are sequestered from relationships that count, they may function as a refuge or retreat, an escape from the tensions and pressures of daily life. Such conflicts and troubles as they produce—and they are as capable of eliciting distress as any relationship—may be somewhat more easily managed because they are encapsulated. Should the relationships become too troubled, they can be dropped without reverberations elsewhere in one's life.

In some ways supplementary relationships may be more responsive to the needs of an individual dealing with chronic deficit than would be the relationships of the individual's ordinary life. Friends are fine in response to crisis, but they become exhausted by chronic distress. Those who provide supplementary relationships are likely to be better able to deal with chronic distress. Indeed, they are likely either to be professionals, whose work requires that they understand, or fellow experiencers, individuals in the same boat themselves.

The primary flaw in supplementary relationships may be their artificiality. The supplementary community of Parents Without Partners exemplifies this problem. Instead of the genuine world of the individual's ongoing work ties, kin ties, friendship networks, there is a world apart, concerned almost solely with the needs of participants. The friendships made within the organization are entirely genuine, the politics are desperately serious, the love affairs are as deep as love affairs can be, and yet the sense of contrivance is inescapable. Perhaps for this reason members in their second year in the organization sometimes speak ruefully of their dependence on it, and members of still longer standing, though they may be grateful for all they gained from it, often express their determination to return, as soon as they can, to life on their own.

When individuals do return to life on their own, the supplementary community is entirely behind them: they have no more contact with its politics and are likely to have moved away from its friendship networks. Their membership was a time out of their lives, like an extended therapeutic cruise.

Relying on
One's Community:
Mrs. Davis

Mrs. Rose Davis was in her late twenties, slim, blonde, and very attractive. She had two children: a girl aged twelve and a boy aged eight. She worked as a typist. Her former husband did not contribute to the support of her children.

When we first met Rose Davis she had been going with Harold, a man about twelve years older than she, for about a year and a half. Harold was separated from his wife but not as yet divorced.

Harold appeared to be devoted to Rose. He frequently gave her gifts of clothes and jewelry and brought toys for the children. He took her shopping and at times went with her to visit her relatives. He spent four or five evenings a week with her, and the remaining evenings he always called.

At that time Rose said about Harold, "We're lucky to have him. He's wonderful to us." Nevertheless, she was unsure about marrying Harold when he gained his divorce. Harold had an ulcer condition, and Rose's boy sometimes upset him. There had already been a stormy scene when Harold spanked the boy and scolded his older sister. The children felt he had exceeded his authority both in punishing them and, earlier, in telling them what to do. Rose defended Harold by saying, "It's all right for Harold to take you everywhere, take you out to dinner, take you to nice places, but if he scolds you, you don't like it." But the incident made her still more uneasy about marriage.

Rose was ambivalent about her sexual relationship with Harold. It meant a great deal to her, yet she was terrified that it would be discovered and that she would be shamed and bring shame to her family. Just before the relationship with Harold ended, she said to the interviewer:

> I'm going to tell you this. I can't tell this to even my own sister. I've been having relations with Harold. Isn't that terrible? Me! I told you how I feel about religion and morals. I've been on pills. Can you imagine it? I had to do something. I don't like a prophylactic or a diaphragm. I never felt they were foolproof. . . . But I'd kill myself if I got pregnant. Do you know what that would do to my family, to my children? When everyone thinks so much of me. My family thinks I am wonderful. . . .
>
> This is why my mother keeps asking me when Harold and I are going to get married. She doesn't like long engagements. She says to me, "Rose, you're such a good girl, I know I don't have to worry about you." But I know she's worried. And I feel like such a hypocrite.

Rose recognized that she could not give Harold up. When he didn't come for dinner she felt the evenings dull and herself dispirited. She began to feel that only with marriage could she have both the relationship and her respectability. Finally she told Harold that they couldn't go on as they had: they would have to go forward to marriage or separate.

A month later, quite without warning, Harold called Rose to say that he had just learned that he could not get a divorce and that he did not think it fair to her to see her again. In addition, he said, his lawyer had advised him to move out of state to escape his wife's financial demands.

When Rose had been eight or nine her father had deserted her family. It is possible that this early loss contributed to the distress she felt at this new abandonment. Her emotional style, too, may have played a role. She tended to express her feelings fully, even exaggerate them, rather than restrain or diminish them; on a scale going from expressive to controlled, she would have been far toward the expressive end. Yet, really, we have no idea what level of intensity of grief would be an appropriate response to so severe a loss. This was her report the next morning:

> I am so miserable and upset. Harold called me and told me that he is leaving the state. His lawyer has advised him to do this. I was so upset after he spoke to me that I cried and cried. In fact I cried over the telephone while he was talking to me. . . . I was so exhausted and so emotionally upset that I didn't sleep during the night. I called in to work and told them I was sick.

One component of the upset was terror at being alone. Only the attachment figure, now lost, could fully have relieved the terror; but some relief could be obtained from another close and sympathetic figure. Rose called her older sister, Isabelle, the sister she was closest to.

> It was very late and I wanted somebody to talk to. I remembered that my sister once said, "Whenever you get upset, no matter what hour it is, call me." So I called her and I spoke with her until 2:30 this morning.

Rose called her mother later that day, and her mother came to see her. Her mother came partly out of a parent's wish to help and partly to express the sympathy of one who had been there herself.

> My mother came and she bawled and we talked. And she felt sorry for him, too, even though she felt so bad for me. She said, "I've been through years when I sat and cried, cried my life away, without Daddy and having you children and everything. And now I see you, with the kids. And it is so hard, how a man can just walk out of your life."

Rose's mother stayed with her that night, and after a time she was able to sleep. Her mother also stayed with her again a week later, just to keep her company.

Others of Rose's near kin also rallied around. Her younger sister Nina stopped by to see her. Nina told her that Harold's love had been genuine. Feeling that she had truly been loved reassured Rose that she was lovable, that she had been right to have felt secure, that she had not been duped. She responded by talking about just how attentive Harold had been, idealizing the relationship in the way new widows idealize their ended marriages:

> My sister Nina came over. She said, "I have no doubts that Harold loved you." She said, "You had a marvelous relationship." You know, of course I could only tell her so much, but I mean everything else I told her about. You know, the things he'd say and the way he'd pick me up and that smile and the way he'd open the door for me. . . ."

Isabelle invited Rose for Sunday dinner, to which she gratefully went. But once there she was reminded that her previous visit had been with Harold, and she broke into tears. A couple of days later she was visited by her younger brother. He was not normally close to her but apparently had been told by others in the family that she was in distress.

My brother came by today. It was good to see him. I made him coffee, and I was on the verge of tears, but I had bawled Sunday at Isabelle's and I just can't keep doing that. I just can't do this every day....

The brother, as had the younger sister, assured Rose that Harold's affection had been genuine.

My brother seemed to understand Harold. He feels that there really isn't anything Harold can do, so why prolong the agony? I mean, he can't offer me marriage.

Rose had two close girl friends, Helen and Toni. Helen was sympathetic enough, though somewhat guarded in her appraisal of Harold's essential commitment. Toni had never liked Harold, possibly because Toni's relationship with Rose had become more distant once Harold appeared on the scene. Toni disparaged Harold; in return Rose disparaged Toni:

Toni couldn't stand him. She didn't even know him and she didn't like him. She said she didn't like his accent. He lived in the South for seventeen years and he has a Southern accent. Yet she goes out with married fellows, goes out to dinner I mean. All her relationships are really nowhere.

After taking one day off, Rose returned to work. But her thoughts were filled with what had happened, and she had neither her usual energy nor her usual good humor.

All last week I wasn't myself in work. I had the bosses telling me, "Come on, Rose, where's your smile?" But I hate to tell you how lost and empty I am.

Work relationships tend to maintain a stable tone no matter what is happening to other aspects of individuals' lives. They have to, if the job is to get done. Private affairs are often discussed at work, but generally in a more matter-of-fact fashion than is possible elsewhere. Co-workers can sympathize with one another, but always there is the shared job to restrain their expressions of feeling. Rose told her boss why she was depressed, and her boss responded in a realistic, if not especially tactful, manner:

I told Mr. Walter that Harold and I were all through. I said that I was really bothered. I said I couldn't help it, and that I knew I'd feel better next week. You know, I'll get over it. But just realizing that we are all through, I feel terrible. But I've got to get over it and I know it. He said, "For a guy who has meant as much to you, I don't see how he can let it go like that. I've got one thing to say about his story: it's bullshit."

Rose received neither support nor understanding from her children. On the contrary, they too were hurt and so became more demanding. The older child in particular wanted to be reassured that the experience of loss would not occur again and again. But Rose had little energy to deal with her children's reactions.

Linda said to me, "First it was Daddy, now it's Harold." And she just said she didn't want to have to think, if I go steady again, that this is what is going to happen. So I said, "I didn't ask for these things either. I wish Daddy had stayed, but he didn't, and I was very hurt too." Harold was hope for me just like he was for them and I certainly didn't ask for this to happen.

Instead of becoming closer to her children and more understanding of them, Rose became extremely short-tempered with the children. She was dismayed by her own behavior, but there seemed little she could do. She tried to explain to the children that she wasn't herself. One evening her daughter became especially demanding—"aggravating" was Rose's term—and Rose exploded with rage, slapped the daughter, and sent her to bed. Two hours later she was overcome with guilt and wrote her daughter a letter of apology.

Almost all of Rose's thoughts and energy were absorbed by obsessional review of the events of her relationship with Harold and what might have been the reasons for its ending. Reminders of Harold seemed everywhere. In shuffling through a drawer she would come on a sweater or a pair of earrings that Harold had given her and stand there, lost in reverie.

I can't believe that I didn't mean something to Harold. He made me feel that I was gorgeous. Everything I see around me makes me think of him. Things he gave me, a gold heart locket last Valentine's Day, the toaster in the kitchen. I open the closet door and there's his sweater, a sweater he gave me.

Sometimes now she questioned whether he really had cared for her:

I keep asking myself, did he really love me or was it an act? If it was an act, he did a hell of a job. He was marvelous to me and the kids.

Rose displayed the symptoms of grief. She cried a great deal. She slept fitfully. She felt chronically depressed. And she felt she simply had to get in touch with Harold again. Despite fear of humiliation, ten days after his call to her she called him.

I called him Wednesday at work, and I told him that it embarrassed me to call, that I don't like to, but that we were more than just friends, what we meant to each other, and that was the reason I was calling. And he said, "Why prolong it?"

And that there was nothing that he could do and there was no future in it. He said that I should pretend that he was a bastard and just forget him. And I said, "How can I pretend you were bad when you were far from it? I just remember all the beautiful things, and I miss hearing your voice and seeing you at the door." And I said how even friends call to say hello. I said, "You should be able to understand how I feel and how hurt I am, because you were so wonderful to me." And after that phone call I bawled a little more. And I just won't call him again. And naturally I feel so lost and empty.

On the Saturday another ten days later, it happened that both of Rose's children were spending the night away from home. The girl was staying with a friend and the boy with Rose's mother. Rose arranged to have dinner with her friend Toni, but then, almost against her will, called Harold's sister to ask if Harold was there. Harold often stopped in to see his sister late on a Saturday afternoon. Harold was not there, and Rose asked the sister to have him call if he should appear. Rose visualized going out for a drink with Harold and the two of them becoming close again and spending the night together. But Harold didn't call, and Rose again felt humiliated.

When Rose now talked about Harold her idealizations were tinctured with anger. She was much more frank about the sexual aspect of their relationship, a frankness that seemed to combine all at once an attempt to recapture a time of warmth and a desire to damage both Harold and herself. Now Rose was willing to describe scenes she once would only allude to:

He was so warm and loving. . . . No matter what we were doing, he would be romantic. Drinking a cup of coffee, watching television, even if I was washing dishes he would come and put his arms around me and give me a kiss on the back of the neck. . . . He knew how to satisfy a woman. Making love with him was beautiful. He would fondle me and I would fondle him. I used to say to him, "Imagine what I could be like if I were your wife and really relaxed."

There was a final letter to Harold in which, for the first time in her communication with him, anger could be discerned. After beginning by saying, "I promise I won't write you or call you any more, but to satisfy my inner self I must write," Rose went on to review how important Harold had been for her and ended by saying, "I'm disappointed at the outcome of our relationship and the fact that it has to end so abruptly. But I could take it a lot better had you allowed it to end with the kindness I was so used to."

It is by no means unusual for anger to appear as a component of grief. Even widows sometimes find reason for anger in their dead spouse's failure to have cared for himself properly. Whether there is rational justification or not, loss of an attachment figure tends to be experienced as abandonment.

About this time many of those close to Rose who had initially supported her idealizations began tincturing their view of Harold with at least mild disapproval. Rose's sister Isabelle began pointing out that Harold had been much older than Rose and that he had also been sick.

Isabelle organized a party and invited both Rose and Ronnie, a man with whom Rose had gone out before Harold came on the scene. Ronnie couldn't make the party because of a business trip, which would take him to another city, but the invitation was enough to let him know that Rose was back in circulation. Ronnie tried to call Rose on his return, but her telephone number was unlisted. He sent her a card and she replied by calling him. They agreed to meet when Ronnie returned from a second business trip. Ronnie never asked about Harold. While on the second trip Ronnie sent Rose a postcard with a photograph of the city he was visiting. Now Rose began remembering the good times she had had with Ronnie:

Ronnie was just a marvelous guy. I gave him up because I wanted to show Harold what a nice girl I was, that I would go steady with him, be his girl.... Of course with Ronnie we never got into any kind of overly warm thing. I mean it was a shake of the hand, a goodnight kiss, "see you later," you know? I could never be that warm with Ronnie. He wasn't that kind of a guy. But I'd sit next to him and we'd dance close and he'd kind of hold me close and that was all right.

Rose's girl friend Helen asked Rose to go with her to a neighborhood nightclub, a place they had been to many times, where they knew the management and the band. They had a nice time, and though Rose remained lonely, her depression lifted for a time.

I ended up going to the Surfside, I had a couple of cocktails there with Helen and heard the guys play. And I had a kiss on the cheek from the leader, who I know. He was so glad to see me. There's no point in staying home and brooding—it just doesn't do any good. I could have very stupidly stayed home, but I think it's only worse to stay home and feel sorry and sick and everything.

About this time Rose was told by her sister Isabelle that Harold had been seen out with another woman. Indeed, he had taken the other woman to a restaurant where one of

Rose's friends worked as a waitress and had introduced her as someone he was going out with. Rose's friend felt unable to tell Rose, but did call Isabelle to tell her. One afternoon when Isabelle was visiting Rose the friend also stopped by. Before leaving she told Rose something like, "I don't think you ought to worry about Harold. I'm sure he's doing fine," after which she nodded significantly to Isabelle. Rose waited until the friend had left and then demanded that Isabelle tell her what it was the friend had been hinting.

When she learned that Harold was going out with someone new Rose felt herself again abandoned. She was again stunned, hurt, and angry.

I only heard it two nights ago. I really haven't had a good cry and I really, really know that I need one. I really do. I mean I'm really shook inside here, you know, and it's all just in my chest, really. But after I heard, I was a wreck. I was really shaking.

Again Rose entered on an obsessional review, this time trying to work out whether Harold could have left her for this other woman, and if so, when he could have possibly met her. Again she slept fitfully. Again she wanted to get in touch with Harold, but now she wanted somehow to get even with him, at the very least to embarrass him. She wrote him a number of notes in which she let him know that she knew, but threw them away. Then, gradually, she found herself caring less.

For some time Isabelle had been telling Rose about a fellow her husband worked with who had had a great deal of trouble in his marriage and was now separated. Isabelle had met the man, whose name was Ed, and liked him. Her husband had worked with Ed for years and knew him to be reliable and sober. Right now he was very lonely. Isabelle thought it would be good for Rose to meet Ed.

Rose was at first unwilling to consider a still-married man. But then she more or less permitted Isabelle to arrange a meeting. It is doubtful that anyone except a near relative would have been so aggressive in intervening in Rose's life.

> My sister kept telling me about this wonderful guy, Ed, works with my brother-in-law, and she'd love me to meet him and just go out with him, because he's such a fine person. Ed is separated. I said, "After Harold I don't want to date anybody unless he's either single or already divorced." I just felt, what if I get to like him, why start something that can't be finished?
>
> Well, to make a long story short the couple downstairs were taking me out for a drink and I mentioned this to my sister. So lo and behold, who came into the place but my sister and my brother-in-law and Ed? So we were all sitting around together and Ed asks me to dance and we all came back to the house for Chinese food and from that night on he started to call.

An attachment formed between Rose and Ed very quickly. Each, of course, was lonely. But this goes only so far in explaining what happened between them. They each must have recognized that the other would somehow do: that the other was someone who could function as a complement to themselves. And they each must have felt enough trust in the other to relinquish their initial wariness. In relation to this, Rose was sure enough of Ed's reliability—because he was essentially recommended by her sister and brother-in-law—to permit herself rather quickly to express, with little hesitancy, the full syndrome of attachment feelings.

We started going out and it just seemed as though— it almost seemed crazy to say we hit it off as well as we did. I just can't believe how I feel about this guy and how he feels about me. Can you believe it? Honest to God, I'm really crazy about him. I can really, honestly, truthfully, say that. . . . I can honestly say that I'm in love with him. I know it. I'm in love with him.

As it happened, this particular story has a happy continuation for at least the year or so after this episode during which we kept in touch with Rose. Ed did get his divorce, and Rose and he were married.

This story may suggest some of the ways in which a natural support structure may help one to endure and then to recover from loneliness. First among Mrs. Davis' resources were her near kin. She could appeal to the closest of these, her older sister and her mother, for reassurance and support. Indeed, she awoke her older sister in the middle of the night and received no rebuke. Her other sister and her brother, when they heard about her loss, let her know that they too were available to her. Friends also rallied around, though they were perhaps less solicitous. Kin and friends together helped her to externalize and to an extent objectify her grief—to treat it as distinct from her, an illness that had happened to her—and in this way supported that part of Mrs. Davis' personality that was struggling to surmount the upset.

Kin and friends also helped Mrs. Davis work out an *account*, a story explaining what had happened. At first they supported Mrs. Davis' idealization of the relationship, while at the same time helping her to define it as over. Then as Mrs. Davis' account changed to admit more ambivalence, kin and friends modified their response appropriately. Eventually they made available new information which required a thorough reconsideration of what had happened. The development of the account was critical, however; with it Mrs. Davis could feel that her world was neither punitive nor arbitrary and though she might have been mistaken in her behavior in the past she could trust herself to manage more effectively in the future.

Mrs. Davis' work relationships offered her a stable structure in which she had a recognized place and made valued contributions. Her sense of worth, severely shaken by Harold's abandonment of her, was partially repaired by the respect in which she was held by her coworkers.

Later Mrs. Davis' sister took a very active role in Mrs. Davis' recovery by bringing her again into contact with an old boyfriend, and though as it happened Mrs. Davis and the boyfriend didn't actually meet, the setting of a tentative date reassured Mrs. Davis regarding her acceptability and attractiveness. She knew that even though there might not be anyone close to her, still she would not be socially isolated. Further reassurance came from invitations to spend the evening with friends and on one occasion to visit a nightclub with a girl friend. It was now that the friendship network let Mrs. Davis know that Harold was seeing someone new. This information desolated her again but also required her to give up hope that Harold would return.

Finally, Mrs. Davis' sister managed to have her meet a co-worker of her husband's. Because this was an introduction arranged by someone in her network, Mrs. Davis knew a great deal about the man, though she had not met him before. He came, as it were, with a vita and a recommendation. And since the man had continuing connections to Mrs. Davis' network, he was under some constraint to behave properly.

The supplementary community that is described in the next section could nearly have matched the provisions of these kin ties, friendship ties, and relationships with co-workers. It could have functioned even more effectively in providing an engaging social life, including opportunites for dating. But Mrs. Davis' reliance on bonds she already had strengthened those bonds. This need not have been the case; others might have felt overburdened by her. But given that Mrs. Davis could rely on her already existent familial and friendship bonds, she emerged from her experience of grief and loneliness better integrated into her community than when she began. This would not have happened had she been forced to rely on a supplementary community or supplementary relationships.

Parents Without Partners as a Supplementary Community

Parents Without Partners (PWP) is by far the largest and best-known organization of single parents. Its aims and program are described in a number of sources.[1] Not all potentially eligible individuals find the organization attractive. Some criticize it as a dating marketplace,[2] though the organization makes every effort to avoid this image. Others do not feel comfortable with the members they encounter in their first explorations of the organization. Nevertheless the organization reported itself in 1971 as having 70,000 members and growing rapidly.[3]

We worked for a bit more than a year with one PWP chapter of about 600 members. During this time we attended most meetings of the Board of Directors, a good many of the frequently held discussion groups, some dances and other

Adapted from Robert S. Weiss, "The Contribution of an Organization of Single Parents to the Well-being of its Members," *Family Coordinator* (July 1973), with permission of the journal's publishers. Work on this study was supported by a grant from the Department of Health, Education, and Welfare, Social and Rehabilitation Service, CRD 294 (2) 7–245, and from the National Institute of Mental Health, 5–RO–1–MH 14528. My collaborator in this study was Professor Carroll Bourg. I am grateful for help from Dr. Donald Klein, Mr. Paul Hochberg, and Mr. Alex Seidler.

social activities, and a few informal parties. We also discussed the organization with many of the more active members and held formal interviews with a small number of current members and former members.

Among the active members there was great variation in needs and interests and, therefore, in patterns of participation. Some gave a great deal of time to administrative work, while others restricted their participation to attendance at discussion groups, and still others were primarily interested in social activities or in programs for children. The pattern of an individual's participation might well change over time. A number of members were at first interested in the discussion groups or social activities but later became more involved in administration.

Members brought many different problems to the organization. Some new members had only just separated from their spouses or, less frequently, had only just been widowed. They often wanted most to have help in managing their immediate upset, perhaps only by having understanding and sympathetic listeners to whom they might talk, perhaps in addition by gaining advice, direction, or support. Most useful for members with these concerns were the discussion groups limited to individuals in similar situations which the organization provided under the general title of "coffee and conversation." In addition, there were therapy groups led by professionals and opportunities to attend lectures dealing with various aspects of the situation of the single parent. Members of longer standing often seemed to have made the transition from marriage to life on their own but to have found that their current lives were unsatisfactory in that important relational provisions were still absent.

The organization seemed to respond in its programming to four types of deficit: (a) the absence of a sustaining community; (b) the absence of friends in similar situations; (c) the absence of support for a sense of worth; and (d) the absence of emotional attachment. Its response to each of these deficits took the form of making available appropriate supplementary relationships.

A SUSTAINING COMMUNITY

Many members had found that as single individuals they felt out of place in their former community. They no longer felt comfortable seeing friends, or, in a few cases, even attending church. On the other hand they felt that in PWP they were among others whose situation was identical to their own; even though they might not at first feel accepted, they were not intrinsically different. Because of this they felt they could come to social events by themselves without embarrassment. Parents Without Partners offered them a chance to get out of their homes.

In recognition of this need, leaders of the organization scheduled events for almost all those times assigned by our society to social activities. These were the times when PWP members might otherwise have been especially likely to feel themselves marginal to the community: weekend evenings, Sunday afternoons, and holidays. Social events were not restricted to these times, but there was an effort to ensure that these times were covered.

The result was an extensive roster of social events. In

one typical winter month there were dance classes, musical groups, Sunday afternoon cocktail parties, a skating party for children and adults and another for adults only, a lecture by a leading psychiatrist on the problems of the single parent, a holiday dance, and several discussion groups.

There were still other activities and events. Administering the organization required meetings to set policy and plan activities. In addition, many members of the organization invited others on an informal basis to dinner or an evening's gathering. It was quite possible for active members to concentrate much or all of their social lives within the organization.

FRIENDS IN THE SAME BOAT

Women, but not men, tended to find PWP valuable because it provided them with the opportunity to form friendships with same-sex others who were in situations similar to their own. Many women seemed to have relinquished friendships they had made during their marriage because of differences in schedules and in concerns, unwillingness to visit in the evening when husbands were home, envy of the married friends, or belief that the married friends feared their attractiveness to the friends' husbands. For these women PWP offered the opportunity to form new friendships with other women in the same boat.

Within PWP, friendships seemed most likely to be established by women of similar age and socioeconomic status who lived near enough to one another to be able to visit occasionally and to exchange such favors as baby-sitting. Not all women were able to find potential friends in PWP, just as PWP was not equally attractive to all single parents who looked it over. Among women who attended a few meetings and then dropped out, the most frequent explanation was that they had not found other women in PWP sufficiently like themselves: the women they had met were the wrong age or too loud or too aggressive or widowed rather than divorced or divorced rather than widowed.

Friendships among a number of women living in the same neighborhood gave rise to cliques which, because their supportive provisions were so important, elicited loyalty. If cliques became rivalrous with one another, as might happen in connection with the competition of members of different cliques for desirable positions in the organization, loyalty to one's own cliques might demand antagonism to the rival clique.

Male friends of clique members tended to be included in the clique as rather marginal members, although at gatherings they might be shown deference and special attention. The female members of the cliques ran them; they were the ones who kept in touch with one another, scheduled parties, decided on guest lists, and in other ways maintained the clique structure.

Some men in the organization formed cross-sex friendships, which were similar in their qualities of loyalty, affection, and exchange of favors to the same-sex friendships of women. Nevertheless, these were largely friendships of convenience. In such a relationship both the man and the woman would understand that a more intense cross-sex relationship, should either of them form one, would lead to a cessation of their contact. In the meantime, the friendship could supply the man with a home to visit where, as one man put it, he could feel a part of a family for a time, and could provide the woman with a masculine presence as well as an escort for an occasional evening out.

Men in the organization exhibited little interest in forming friendships with one another. Leaders in the organization had learned from experience that an all-male activity, such as an evening of poker or a bowling tournament, would be sparsely attended. Men who were in administrative roles in the organization sometimes developed a sense of comradeship—when they were not actively rivalrous—but they would meet only when required to by their organizational responsibilities. When they did meet they often discussed personal as well as organizational issues.

SUPPORT FOR A SENSE OF WORTH

Both men and women sometimes found that contribution to the organization through administrative or planning roles supported their own sense of worth. Leaders referred to this phenomenon by saying, "The more you put into PWP, the more you get out of it." There were at least three ways in which individuals benefited through their contribution to the organization. First, they established a place for themselves in the organization and so facilitated further participation. A woman who was chairman of a dance committee remarked that it was only because she was in charge that she had the courage to attend. Second, the effective management of an organizational task reassured members of their general competence, a quality that the failure of their marriages had led many of the separated and divorced to doubt. And finally, successful completion of an organizational task was rewarded by both formal and informal praise, which contributed to increased self-esteem. One woman, just elected to an important office, said at the Installation Dinner, "I can say what PWP has given me in just one word: worthwhileness."

It was recognized within the organization that opportunity for leadership was itself one of the benefits of membership. Perhaps for this reason the organization included almost two dozen administrative divisions, such as "cultural programs," "recreational programs," and "children's activities." This administrative fragmentation made it possible for leaders to offer many members a position of some responsibility, if not as a director, then as program coordinator or other functionary within a division.

Contributions to the organization were generally acknowledged in the monthly bulletin. As a consequence, the bulletin carried many stories praising, congratulating, and at the least naming members who had in some way earned notice. Members felt hurt if their contributions went unrecognized, but generally leaders were careful, even in informal conversation, to allocate credit generously.

The same needs that led to the importance among members of recognition for service led to great sensitivity among them to criticism. Unfortunately, distrust of other members of the organization, sometimes because they were members of rival cliques, made for readiness to criticize. Every year determined and angry criticism led to resignations from the Board of Directors. One year, it was reported, half the original board resigned.

Nevertheless, the benefits of leadership were believed to

outweigh the risks involved. The benefits were thought especially great for men. Virtually every man who appeared reasonably competent was pressed to accept an administrative position. Women, on the other hand, might have to assume greater initiative; one woman said it had taken her almost a year to get the organization's inner circle to allow her to direct the discussion group program. But if a woman was persistent she would probably be successful; here, for example, despite the initial reluctance of the leadership, the woman was ultimately permitted to assume responsibility for an important organizational activity.

A NEW EMOTIONAL ATTACHMENT

Most members, even those who had voluntarily ended their marriages, experienced loneliness prior to joining PWP. It was widely believed in the organization that hope of respite from loneliness was the reason most members had joined the organization. But the friendships among women and collegial relationships among men that PWP sponsored seemed only to mitigate, not to dispel, loneliness. Speaking of the slight value of friendships for dealing with loneliness, one woman said, "Sometimes I have the girls over and we talk about how hard it is. Misery loves company, you know."

For most members only cross-sex attachments could effectively fend off loneliness. Many of those who were lonely, as well as many coming to the organization at least partly because of loneliness, hoped to establish such an attachment, to find someone to date with whom they might eventually become involved.

Despite these motivations of members, the organization was presented forcefully to the public and to new members as not being concerned with the diminution of loneliness. The following description of the organization's goals, given by an officer in an orientation meeting for prospective members, is typical of such presentations: "This is not a lonely hearts club.... This is primarily so we can discuss problems about raising children. And if you can contribute and become a worker, then you will get so much more out of it."

In another orientation meeting a prospective member who said that he hoped he might find dates in the organization was sharply reproved with the statement, "If you are here for dating, this is not for you."

Nevertheless, the chapter sponsored dances and parties which seemed designed primarily to provide members with opportunities to meet possible dates. The parties were generally restricted to members or to members and their guests, but single men not members of the chapter were invited to the dances since otherwise the four-to-one preponderance of women in the chapter would have made for an uncomfortably unbalanced sex ratio. The possibility of meeting someone whom one might date was implicit in this activity—as, in truth, it was in every activity that involved both men and women. Members recognized this and expressed their recognition in almost every mixed activity by jokes, innuendo, and alertness to any indication of genuine sexual or romantic interest in themselves or in others.

Almost all men who had been with the organization for longer than six months seemed at some point to have dated a woman within the organization. From comments made in discussion groups it appeared that more than a fourth and perhaps as many as a half of the female members who had been in the organization for more than six months had dated men who were members. These are impressions, but there appeared to be a good deal of dating within the organization.

Nevertheless, the leaders of the organization adamantly refused to acknowledge that the organization provided members with possible dating partners. Dances and parties were rationalized as necessary recreation. Leaders insisted that most members were not yet "ready" to get involved with others, despite their knowledge that many were actively seeking just such involvement, and some had already found it.

Why did the leaders adopt this strategy? Why did they refuse to acknowledge that much of the organization's program was directed to providing settings in which members might explore the possibility of establishing emotionally significant cross-sex relationships?

One important reason was the belief held by leaders that only if PWP insisted that it did not sponsor dating could it attract respectable individuals to membership. An ex-president of the organization suggested that before the achievement of public acceptance of the sobriety of PWP's mission, membership in the organization and even more so in its leadership had been stigmatizing. He said: "I wouldn't accept the presidency for years. There was a stigma attached to it because of this lack of understanding of PWP in the community. You used to say Parents Without Partners and they would giggle."

Leaders were less concerned with actually discouraging

dating than with preventing the identification of the organization with the promotion of dating. They could tolerate dating among members, indeed date themselves and gossip about the dating patterns of others, so long as the dating was understood as distinct from any organizational activity. It was essential that individuals not be obviously in search of potential dates when engaged in an organizational activity—dances and parties to an extent excepted—and that individuals who were dating conduct themselves with circumspection. So long as dating could be treated as nonorganizational it could be managed.

For still other reasons, besides their concern for the organization's—and their own—good name, it was important to many individual members to be able to claim that they had joined PWP for reasons quite apart from the hope of finding someone to date. Men could in this way defend themselves from the suspicion that they were insufficiently attractive or resourceful to have found dates on their own. Some men went further than simply saying that they had not joined PWP for dates; they insisted that they had been fully occupied before joining PWP and after joining had made it a practice not to date within the organization. Many women in the organization, though they might in private frankly discuss their loneliness, would have felt threatened, almost assaulted, if they were to believe they had inadvertently entered an organization that was more than anything else a dating marketplace. A minority of women, almost all of them widows, had sincerely given up the possibility of forming another attachment. Organizational dissimulation in different ways helped all these members feel more comfortable in their membership.

THE PROBLEMS OF AN ORGANIZATION THAT FUNCTIONS AS A SUPPLEMENTARY COMMUNITY

Organizations that provide supplementary communities are liable to certain difficulties in meeting purely organizational aims, since efficiency and even certainty of survival as an organization must sometimes be compromised in the interests of contribution to the well-being of its members.

In PWP, because responsibility was seen as a potential benefit of membership, there were more positions of responsibility than necessary, resulting in difficulties in coordination. Turnover in leadership was expected and in some positions (the presidency for one) required, and individuals were sometimes appointed or elected in the belief that the position would be good for them, although usually there was also some basis for assurance that they would perform with at least minimal adequacy.

Another source of inefficiency and friction was the organization's sponsorship of friendships and friendship networks, which resulted in its sometimes appearing to be a loose confederation of rivalrous cliques rather than a single entity. An organization concerned with efficiency could not tolerate the priority of friendships over organizational commitments. But in PWP the friendship relationships were among the very aims of the organization.

Still another source of strain within PWP was its responsiveness to the loneliness of its membership, although responsiveness conceivably threatened the survival of the organization. Potential members were sometimes frightened off and present members made diffident about their membership by the occasional eruption into obviousness of attachment needs.

Yet the organization continued, uneasily, to provide opportunities to meet these needs.

Few members of PWP recognized how many difficulties were encountered by the organization in its attempt to function as a supplementary community. For many members the problem of membership often came rather from recognition of the artificialty of the community. They might be grateful for the existence of PWP yet at the same time resentful of their need for it and critical of its limitations.

Some members said they hoped that the time would come when they would no longer have to concentrate their social life within PWP. They recognized that PWP was supplementary in the sense that they had joined it because of deficits in their lives created by the loss of a marriage, the fading of friends, the erosion of their place in their community. To belong to PWP required that they acknowledge the need to make do, if only temporarily, with something other than their real lives.

NOTES

1. See Elizabeth E. Harris, "Parents Without Partners, Inc.: A resource for clients," *Social Work* 11 (1966): 92–98; Ethel P. Gould, "Special Report: The single-parent family benefits in Parents Without Partners, Inc.," *Journal of Marriage and the Family* 30 (1968): 666–671; Patricia N. Clayton, "Meeting the needs of the single-parent family," *The Family Coordinator* 20 (1971): 227–336; and James Egleson and Janet Frank Egleson, *Parents Without Partners* (New York: Dutton, 1961).

2. See Morton M. Hunt, *The World of the Formerly Married* (New York: McGraw-Hill, 1966), p. 88.

3. Clayton, "Meeting the needs."

7

Conclusion:
Summary and Implications
for Further Study

The materials presented here have touched on a good many issues related to the central theme of loneliness. They have considered the symptomatologies of loneliness and have offered explanations for them. They have considered the conditions that give rise to loneliness, the "feel" of loneliness, and the ways individuals attempt to manage loneliness. What may be learned from these materials?

It seems to me to be reasonably well demonstrated that loneliness is a deficit condition, a response to the absence of specific relational provisions. The deficit is always one of a specific provision or provisions. It is not possible for an individual to compensate for the absence of one relational provision by increased acquisition of others; to put it another way, relational provisions cannot be substituted for one another. Thus someone whose life is without emotional attachment cannot compensate for this deficit by throwing himself into his work or entering into more active relations with friends or devoting himself to his children; despite his participation in these latter social activities and engagements, he would remain lonely.

Two deficit states, one which I have named emotional isolation and another which I have named social isolation, seem to occur with some frequency in our society. Each seems to give rise to a syndrome experienced as loneliness, although the syndromes are not identical to one another. Each syndrome does, however, include among its elements extreme discomfort, sometimes reaching the level of pain. Whether the loneliness of emotional isolation is the more severe affliction is difficult to say; it sometimes appears so, but we have no good evidence one way or another.

Loneliness, inasmuch as it is a deficit state, would not be expected to fade with time. Still there is some indication (in Townsend's data) that those who have experienced emotional isolation for a truly extended period—five years or longer—may complain less of loneliness than those whose emotional isolation has been of shorter duration. It seems to me unlikely that individuals can adapt to either emotional isolation or social isolation in the sense that their lives can be satisfactory despite these deficits. But it does seem to me to be possible that individuals might in time change their standards for appraising their situations and their feelings, and, in particular, that standards might shrink to conform more closely to the shape of a bleak reality.

There is no time in one's life when loneliness ceases to be a threat. On the contrary, it appears that one of the risks of aging is an increased vulnerability to loneliness. The aged, like the rest of us, require the provisions of social relationships, but more than the rest of us stand in risk of losing relationships to death or to the vagaries of their own, their friends' or their children's changing circumstances.

These are in my opinion the highlights of what we know

CONCLUSION: SUMMARY AND IMPLICATIONS

about loneliness. **There is much more about which we as yet** have too little understanding.

We still lack a secure taxonomy of types of loneliness. **This** book has focused on two types that seem widespread but has noted that there are others. We need more understanding of the implications of separation from children and from kin. It is possible, although I think unlikely, that there are varieties of loneliness that are not responses to deficit conditions. This would be worth checking; are there times when even those whose lives are in every way adequate nevertheless experience loneliness?

We are just beginning to identify situations at risk of loneliness and to establish the numbers of individuals in various situations who experience loneliness. We can go much farther with the survey method than we have as yet. We can try to learn about the frequencies of loneliness of differing intensity and duration, the distributions of particular symptomatologies, and the conditions under which, despite situations of risk, loneliness is escaped. And surely we can find better ways of establishing the existence and measuring the intensity of loneliness than the single brief question on which our surveys have thus far relied.

We know as yet very little about characterological propensity toward loneliness. There are a number of questions in this area that deserve study. Are there character types, or ways of life, or deep commitments that are more likely than others to bring individuals to situations of risk and are therefore more likely eventually to lead to loneliness? Are there individuals who, given conditions of deficit, experience greater pain, find the deficit more difficult to tolerate, and who are more liable to personality disorganization? Does it matter, in relation to susceptibility to loneliness and capacity to tolerate loneliness, whether one has experienced loss in one's early years? And if it matters, does early loss make one more or less likely to escape loneliness and to be able to manage it should it occur?

Another issue is that of the long-term effects of loneliness, both social and physical. Is there any permanent change in the way in which someone who has experienced extended loneliness later integrates new relationships? And what is the impact of loneliness on those of an individual's relationships that continue intact despite deficit in some other sector—on his or her work ties, relationships with kin, relationships with children? Is there any physical damage because of the extended stress—expressed in sleeplessness, tension, and irritability—that seems often to accompany loneliness?

Finally, what can we do to help individuals cope with loneliness? Can we somehow prepare those who are likely to encounter loneliness—one thinks of those who know their marriages are about to end—so that the experience is not so devastating? Can we somehow devise new forms of social organization, or support those that are now being developed, that reduce the likelihood of situations where we now identify risk? One thinks of the aged, some of whom now seem condemned to loneliness until their deaths. Do retirement communities work? Or are they simply waiting rooms for passing on? What alternatives have been devised, and what is their value?

There has been much speculation that ours is a society that

CONCLUSION: SUMMARY AND IMPLICATIONS

by its very assumptions produces repeated situations of risk.[1] If this is so, we might support social change, perhaps especially change in a communitarian direction. Yet one suspects that even in communes there may be loneliness as couples change partners or as, for any number of reasons, individuals leave. It may be that loneliness is intrinsic in the human condition, that there is an irreducible minimum level of risk below which we simply cannot go. Very likely American society as it is now constituted presents more risk than this. But how much more, and what would it cost us in our ability to realize whatever may be our aims for ourselves to achieve how much reduction?

Let us turn now from this review of still unexplained areas to consider what may be the implications of what we do know for those who are currently suffering from loneliness or who may in the future suffer from loneliness. As I have indicated, this is a group that may reasonably be supposed to include almost all of us. To draw implications for behavior from observations requires, of course, that one introduce one's values. Other observers, with values different from mine, might draw different implications.

I can offer no method for ending loneliness other than the formation of new relationships that might repair the deficit responsible for the loneliness. And I think this solution ordinarily is not easy. If it were, there would be fewer lonely people.

I cannot join with those who suggest that one cherish one's loneliness, that one treat it as a test of moral fiber or as a vision quest or as a demonstration of one's singularity. I think this proposal is a recommendation that one rise above one's genuine feelings, but distance above is distance nevertheless. The proposal would have one develop a rather mystical misrepresentation of one's discomforts, alienating oneself from their actual character, and so making it more difficult to deal intelligently with them, all in the interest of a flimsy and self-congratulatory denial. To dwell on one's loneliness may overburden one's relationships with those who are not lonely. The lonely may have to recognize this and choose with discretion the times and places they will permit their loneliness to show. But tact is very different from self-delusion; indeed, the two may not be compatible.

If one is indeed dealing with emotional or social isolation, all that one can do in the short term is to learn to tolerate the natural loneliness one must feel. This certainly does not mean learning not to feel it, nor even learning not to act on it; the first is impossible, the second sometimes nearly so. But it does mean that when the evening comes, if instead of being able to settle down with a good book it is absolutely necessary to get out or to call a friend who is likely to understand or to write a too-emotional letter that may or may not be sent, that one permit oneself to behave in the way one must, that one maintain some understanding and some generosity toward oneself. It also means that one recognize that there is no cause for panic, no need to imagine that emotional disaster has left one's life forevermore crippled. Things can get better. This does not make them better *now,* but it is nevertheless essential to keep this rather strong possibility in mind.

Yet for things truly to get better requires the re-establishment of linkages, the end of isolation. How does one manage this? It may be useful to begin to respond to this natural question by considering separately the loneliness of social isolation and the loneliness of emotional isolation.

It is my impression that if one's interests and outlook and commitments are like those of others in a social network and if one maintains proximity to that network—stays in touch with its members—that in most cases it is only a matter of time until one is accepted as a member oneself. The time required for acceptance may in some circumstances seem unconscionably long, as has been the experience of some women who with their families moved into conservative and long-established neighborhoods. And occasionally it happens that one's nationality or ethnicity or whatever makes one unacceptable no matter what, as has been the experience of members of a variety of ethnic, racial, and religious groups all over the world. But generally proximity makes for acceptance.

The problem, then, in relation to social isolation is to locate a group or network of adequately attractive and congenial others and manage to stay in touch with at least some of its members long enough to establish membership oneself. There are any number of ways in which this can be done— through setting up social occasions with individuals met through work or through one's spouse's work, through participation in enterprises such as newcomers' clubs or church groups, through classes or interest groups. I may be mistaken, but it seems to me that once the problem is identified and once one makes up one's mind to manage it, social isolation can be combatted effectively, though perhaps some patience may be required before the deficit is finally repaired.

Emotional isolation is more difficult to manage. One may possibly hope for help from those in one's natural support system, as did Mrs. Davis. But suppose they fail to help? One might attempt to form supplementary relationships with a therapist or counselor. This can allay loneliness, but it is temporary, may be costly, and is hardly an adequate source of provisions of attachment. Yet to embark on a campaign of search for an attachment figure is a questionable enterprise simply in terms of likelihood of success, quite apart from the problems such a campaign might raise in connection with one's self-image.

Where would one look? One might try the usual devices for "meeting someone"—the "singles groups" that are maintained by churches as well as by bars seeking a free-spending clientele, the consultation of amateur or professional matchmakers or date-arrangers. If one works at the search there are likely to be meetings and dates and eventually, as Mrs. Graham characterized it, an involvement. But my guess is that the relationships that develop are thinly based and fragile and that a likely experience is repetitive loss.

One reason that active search for attachment is risky is, I suspect, that it often requires that one act outside one's social context and meet others who are acting outside theirs. There is both support and constraint in the relationships ordinarily maintained with kin, friends, co-workers, neighbors, and the others who people one's relational life. Acting outside the context they provide may facilitate sexual adventure—although it may also make one wary—but it provides little basis for trust or for trustworthiness.

In addition, it seems unlikely that someone met by chance in a "singles" context will share values and commitments to a degree sufficient to sustain more than a few long conversations. Someone introduced by friends at least has membership in one's social milieu; but someone met by chance could be from anywhere in our variegated society.

Finally, because meetings outside of one's usual social context have so poor a prognosis for long-term survival, they are likely to be defined from the beginning as brief encounters. And this too contributes to their fragility.

Insofar as these impressions are correct, I would think it poor strategy to attempt to deal directly with the loneliness of emotional isolation by putting great energy into "finding someone." It would be more useful to accept that one's loneliness may last for some time—how long may be a matter of pure chance—but that in any event there are distinct limitations to one's ability to remedy the deficit that is its cause.

Yet it seems to me that there is something constructive one can do: direct one's energy to projects, friendships, groups one cares about. This is not quite advising that one keep busy, although there is something to be said for that advice too. Rather it is advising that one develop relationships with others, engagements with activities, memberships in networks, on bases valid in themselves. Then it may well happen that a potential attachment figure will be encountered in connection with these social activities. And because it will then be someone who is within a milieu in which one also has membership, the many problems of attachments outside of social contexts will be avoided.

It may be well, however, to recognize that under the pressures of emotional isolation one's range of acceptable others tends to broaden. The great need for attachment among the very lonely can lead to inappropriate and potentially troublesome choices.

This is all the advice I have to give. But having now presented it I am aware of how uncomfortable I feel about having assumed the role of advisor to the lonely. There is something undignified, indeed faintly comic, about the role: Dear Abby, Miss Lonelyhearts. But this is itself an interesting phenomenon. Why should this be the case? I doubt if I would feel so vulnerable to derision if I were offering advice to the unemployed. Indeed, this discomfort must be among the reasons for the paucity of serious attention to loneliness. And it may suggest, again, that one of the burdens of loneliness is that we have so many preconceptions regarding its nature, so many defenses against recognizing its pain, and so little knowledge of how to help.

NOTE

1. See especially Philip Slater, *The Pursuit of Loneliness* (Boston: Beacon Press, 1970).